DISCOVER THE ESSENTIALS
OF
MULTI-LEVEL MARKETING
AND
THE ESSENTIALS
OF
TIME MANAGEMENT

BY

WARREN BROWN

GOLDCOPY PUBLICATIONS
LONDON
2012

Copyright@Warren Brown. London. 2012

ISBN 978-1-291-22097-1

GOLDCOPY PUBLICATIONS

All rights reserved. No part of this book may be reproduced or transmitted in any form or by any means, electronic or mechanical, including photo-copying, recording or by any information storage and retrieval system without permission in writing from the Publisher.

OTHER BOOKS BY WARREN BROWN
The Secret Race Anglo-Indians
World Recipes for a High Income Business
Discover Parallel Universes
The Anglo-Indian Race Preservation Course
The Lady of the Sea and other Poems

Acknowledgments

To all those who assisted me with the research work
for this book.

The Multi Level Marketing Concept

The concept of multi level marketing can simply be associated with the scenarios you see in the normal world of corporate offices - where the top line typically consists of managers, supervisors, and CEOs – except that in the former, the pyramid can be the other way around. Sounds confusing, isn't it? However, that is exactly how multi level marketing is. It means that in the multi level marketing environment, those on the bottom lines can be at the top, depending on how they work hard to achieve the success they want in this business.

The Pyramid Line

In the corporate world, every position in the pyramid has different salary from the others. In order that the person in the lower rank climbs up the top spot, there are obstacles to be successfully conquered. If they don't do it the right way, they remain in that lower spot and have no chances of earning high salary range like the top bosses do. On other issue, the top position is followed by four slots, followed by more slots, until a pyramid is completed to indicate the work team in a certain corporate office.

In the multi level marketing companies, it is a perfect pyramid line where there is one on topmost position, two on the next, four on the next, and so on and so forth. The person on the top position is actually the first recruiter and the top earner. However, unlike in the corporate world, everyone on the pyramid is their own bosses and everybody has fair chances to earn huge amounts of money, depending on how much work and success they take along the path. This means that even the person on the lowest spot can still reach the top as far as financial freedom is concerned.

Investment, Financial Freedom, and Family Tree

The first thing that you do is invest certain amount of money to build your own line. After a certain time, you can earn money by recruiting down line members and even more money when they too recruit their own down line members. If you work harder, there are more chances of you earning higher. You just need to train and motivate the people on your down line so that they too work harder until your own organization chart is created and has become bigger. The good thing about this is it can keep growing and growing, and your income increasing and increasing too.

The pyramid in multi level marketing is not about the status of the members but their tenacity to claim the financial freedom that they always wanted. Everybody is entitled to become richer, so long as they work hard for it. The best thing about it is there is never an ending cycle to everybody on the pyramid as it continues to grow from generations to generations. And though it is the prime motive of all, it can not be all about the money itself.

As the cycle continues to grow bigger, the bonds between each down line and up line are formed too enabling them to build better relationship; thus, being able to work better with each one.

And so, the concept of multi level marketing can be just perfect for everybody who wants to have financial freedom that can last a lifetime and as well as have a family which supports each other.

What Is There About Multi Level Marketing?

Everyone is doing multi level marketing due to promises of financial freedom. There have been lots of stories emerging from different people who have been involved. The concept is very simple and easy to understand. You invest money to become a business owner or distributor of products or services and earn money from commissions or profit from your sales. Residual profit supplements your income as your team or down line makes sales too. The bigger that your team gets over time, the more chances of you and the members earning huge income. Income increases exponentially over the years so long as your team continues to grow.

Multi level marketing companies are often made popular over word of mouth. Friends, family, contact friends, associates, and others are usually prospects that distributors target to become their down line. However, it may sound easy convincing these prospects but it may take more time and hard work. That is why, a course of action must be properly planned before going over and encouraging people to join and sign up. One way to do is to list all the prospects. Then, one by one, or maybe a group, contact them to introduce the product or service and present the business plan. With proper execution of sales talking, plus luck, they will sign up.

As you go experiencing doing these tasks, you will discover and learn other strategies to use to get more prospects signing up. More of them will not interpret the potential of your business model that easily while most end up refusing than signing up. It can be very discouraging at times, and may even leave you believing it is not cut out for you. But it is the real challenge of multi level marketing business.

In reality, you have to work harder and talk to more and more people and show them the plan and potentials. All successful network marketers have endured it all. With hard work and determination, there is no reason that you shouldn't get that trophy of this game too. It has to be constant and you have to be persistent in encouraging people to become distributors and recruiters. Sitting back at home and dreaming of financial success will never get you there.

Three Pointers

1.) Time commitment. It will take time to build your own organizational chart, or more like the pyramid, to get that cash really flowing big time. If you are really serious about multi level marketing business, have one person at the least to talk to and present with your business plans every day. It will just leave you enough time to tend to your other daily responsibilities but still getting that chance of recruits.

2.) Cold contacting. After you exhausted the people close to you, it is time to figure out other people not in the list. You can have referrals and these people may not be of one of your personal contacts. This can be the more difficult as you need to talk to them without looking as if you are hunting them down just to present your business plans and potentials of them earning big money too.

3.) Weeding out your prospects. It is a good idea to contact first those people who you think have the same interest in plunging into the business and dream of achieving financial freedom. Just remember to take note that there are no easy ways to learn unless you talk to them first.

Multi Level Marketing Essential Facts

Multi level marketing, or MLM, has become popular since it was introduced more than 50 years ago and until now many companies are using it to boost their financial growth. The remarkable thing about this business strategy is that it has helped not only the company itself but many people as well in terms of monetary success.

If you too are interested in joining the field, by hard work, it will never be impossible for you to reach that success status too. To do it, check the following facts and tips to get you familiarized around the whole concept of multi level marketing.

Diligence Is the Key

Before signing up with a company, learn everything about it first. You don't want to deal with a company that doesn't have legal documents that indicate it is legitimately operating in the business. Experts would suggest you look for companies that already earned a good reputation and excellent track record.

They should also be in existence in the industry for long, at least five or more years. Be sure that they have an abundance of supply of their product. And finally, check their policies and make sure you understand them particularly on the aspect of how they pay the members.

It Needs More Time

If you don't have enough time to allot to this particular endeavor, you are not going to make it on top. This is because joining an MLM business group entails attending regular meetings, marketing schedules, and other business activities, which all allow you to interact with your prospects.

Aside from that, a lot of time will be spent attending seminars and following up on your prospects. While there are some people who say MLM can be done on a spare time, more time is of the essence if you want to earn huge real financial rewards.

Rejection is Normal

You may have hundreds of prospects in your list. However, take note that there could be only one in a hundred who will be willing to sign up and work with your team. So, make sure you are prepared to do the whole lot of work and take rejection as vital part of the entire game. Being a good sport will allow you to continue without losing your drive to succeed.

It Involves Selling

Whether you like it or not, selling tangible products or services is part of a legitimate multi level marketing business. In fact, if the company you come across claims you don't have to sell a single thing in order to earn money, it will pay later for you to walk out.

Either it is a scam or it is intentionally omitting this part from your training in order to easily convince you. Either which, multi level marketing may not be for you if you believe you won't succeed by being a salesman.

It Needs a Good Exit Strategy

Multi level marketing business yields low risk yet high financial rewards; however, it is a good idea to see it as a good, short-term investment. There may be other people who have sustained their earnings for years; the truth is not all people have done it only for a year or a little more but never long.

This is not to say that you will never achieve long-term financial success with MLM; however, unless you believe you know how to sustain your income from MLM business, it is important to be prepared with a good exit strategy to avoid financial downfall.

Multi Level Marketing: You Can Be A Financial Success!

The multi level marketing strategy has already been proven so many times in the industry, so how come that there are still many people failing while others are making insane amounts of income?

- Just like in any other adventure, only those people who give up that can fail in MLM industry.

They give up because of two things:

- They are not up to rejections; or
- They get easily tired after seeing slow results

Multi level marketing is that business opportunity in which consultants or affiliates (the members/dealers) are being compensated with commissions they make not only from their sales of the products but also from the sales of the other team members who were referred down through different network levels.

However, as brilliant business concept as it is most members end up leaving before they even have the chance to earn huge amount of money. Perhaps, the most common reason for this is that people don't believe in the marketing part of the MLM. Wherein, in order to become a success in this industry, you have to master the art of marketing, which is keeping people interested and recruiting them so that it is not only but they too earn income.

Rejection and Generating Leads

It is probably a mistake by some MLM companies to miss out the very important part of the marketing at the very start, which is generating leads for more lists of prospects. So, for the reason of lack of good prospects, people get frustrated and not continue with the business.

If the company omits this important detail, it is most likely a sure thing that the members will lose their motivation too at a later part of the campaign. Therefore, MLM companies should be aware that it was never a good move.

Similarly, it is never an effective marketing if people are not trained well in terms of generating leads and orienting them about possible rejections being part of the entire process.

Because of the shortcoming, what normally happens is when the new members start recruiting and hearing rejection after a few phone calls. At first, they may react without hard feelings but as it continues to be like that, they easily grow wary and doubtful.

This is so true even to the people who were very determined at first. If they are not trained or oriented enough, they easily lose that determination and quit thinking multi level marketing is not cut out for them. If they start running out of potentials in the list, they start panicking.

All these scenarios can be eliminated if the multi level marketing company provides all the business resources and tools necessary for the invitation, presentation, and the selling processes. In this way, the members will find it easier to work with the whole program without having the need to quit at any part of the entire game.

Also, it will help them not see rejections as a negative part but a motivation to continue doing the tasks as required to being financial success. If done in the right manner, the MLM members will continue even if confronted with lack of progress at the start because they knew that a steady flow of prospects is available and interested.

A multi level marketing company can have so many effective ways to apply that marketing art. It is just a matter of applying different mediums and making sure the marketing strategy is most useful and valuable to the members so they don't feel being left out at any part of the business game.

What You Need To Know About Multi Level Marketing

For the uninitiated, multi level marketing is not entirely new to the business. In fact, it has been around the industry for more than half a century ago when it was introduced in the United States by a company, which, at the time was marketing nutritional supplement via this strategy better known as the network marketing. The main concept is to combine direct selling and franchising in one marketing plan. All the participants are encouraged to do both tasks in order to earn more money than by merely selling the merchandise.

How Does It Work?

Basically, the participants need to recruit additional members at the same time as they need to supply the products. By doing so, they earn commissions on top of the sale price. But multi-level marketing does not promise big profit from merely selling the products as members have the potentials to earn more from encouraging other people to signup and work hard to recruit others too until a pyramid-like group is formed. They are typically required to buy the products or services but they have to recruit at least two members to earn commissions from their purchased products.

The person on top earns commissions from their down lines the same way as the second, third, and so on and forth, from their down lines. Obviously, people who join this marketing group have high chances of earning larger profit if they have recruits or down lines or the latter continues to recruit new members too. Existing and the new members are considered the distributors and end users of the products or services.

Criticisms and Issues

Because of the rampant cases of business scams, the true essence of multi level marketing business model has been ignored as a true legitimate and significant marketing plan not only in the United States but in the global economy. The scheme was criticized due to the questionable process of recruitment where the members acquire their profit and revenue. It was in the 1980s when it further built a negative reputation when various companies allowed members to focus on marketing and neglected the need to distribute or stock the products.

It has resulted to the illegal pyramid scams, which resemble the legitimate multi level marketing concept, minus the product. While legitimate multi level marketing strategy has genuine scheme, pyramid schemes often are too good to be true that they inevitably collapse in the end because the company has become unable to compensate the exponential growth of newer investors.

Major Change

Because of the increase of the people becoming victims to illegal multi level marketing schemes, a major change was seen in the 1980s, when companies have begun performing the marketing strategy in a different way. Nowadays, they do it by recruiting new members, taking their orders, shipping the goods, paying the earned commissions, and then taking orders again from their members or clients.

Caution

If you have the intention to be involved in a multi-level marketing business to earn huge sum of compensation, it is vital that you know what company you are trying to become a member of. It would be a wise move to investigate the background and the capability of that company to pay the members. Doing the necessary measures is imperative to avoid you from becoming one of the unfortunate victims of pyramid scams.

Do You Need Multi Level Marketing Software?

Running a multi level marketing (MLM) group is just like running a traditional business company. You need to see to it that profits are increasing the same time as sales are soaring. You also have to ensure out of stock products are replaced in time and orders are being taken cared of properly. Furthermore, you need to keep track of all the members of business group so you ensure they are all in the right direction.

All these tasks sound simple but in actuality, it is a different story. That is the reason why you need to have something to organize the complete selling and marketing process of your products.

And nowadays when everything has submitted to the wonders of the high digital era, what better medium to hire than good, dependable multi level marketing software? It is the thing that can not only help you keep track of your MLM genealogy, products' stock, and sales lead, but more importantly, it helps reduce, or possibly, avoid errors and discrepancies as well as improvise your business strategy so to accentuate sales.

But the question is: where do you get the right multi level marketing software?

Do you have to purchase it from the internet or software provider?

Or do you have to hire a software programmer and develop it for you? Read the following to be enlightened of this dilemma.

Both are great options; however, the real answer to those questions is to be extremely careful when choosing software or provider. If you choose to hire a programmer, you may want to ensure he is the right hand for your needs. You don't want to end up with a young, enthusiastic, cocky programmer who can start giving you ideas of success results but can not do it in the end.

It can place your sound business down the drain, so it is very important that the hand you hire knows how to do it, understands what you want, perfectly comprehends the type of problem, draws the solution to it, and cooperate with you.

Inexperienced programmers are one of them you should not trust. As inexperienced as they are, they don't know the real score of what's happening in the business, thus, are unable to give the real solutions to your need. Those who are abreast with the technical advances and latest technology can be your right candidates as they most likely know the ups and downs of your business. No matter what, be sure to do the right thing by screening out all the resumes on your table and asking the applicants all questions relevant to their qualifications and capability.

It is the same if you choose to get a provider. You need to screen out the best software if you don't want to put thousands of dollars into waste. Software are often expensive, so be vigilant with your search. Choosing a provider with thousands of hours of experience is one key to finding the right solution. You can research on this matter over the internet and better yet, from those people who have the authority over software knowledge, specifically multi level marketing software.

Whether you are hiring a programmer or buying multi level marketing software provider to help you run your business, it will help best to remember the above ideas. Remember that you are finding the right solution for your business to make it stronger and smarter. Check all their claims, be patient and ask around.

You will soon find out the right software that answers to your needs, specifically a program that keeps real-time.

Multi Level Marketing: Generating Leads

Is your monthly income not sufficient that you find yourself frequently not meeting ends? Have you considered becoming a multi level marketing distributor? Do you know it can make you more money and build your own business?

Multi level marketing is a business system in which consumer products are sold by the distributors who have signed up with the company. The distributors have the option to sell a minimum or more amount of products each month to generate commissions.

Or they don't have to sell at all, just purchase the required initial amount, but have to recruit enough dealers, who also need to buy or sell a minimum amount of products, to earn the commissions.

Recruiting new dealers or distributors is the main agenda of the multi level marketing business system. People have to go out with a list of prospects to encourage them to join the business group.

But the problem nowadays with this system is that more people have grown wary of the pyramid scams, which were actually patterned after the successful MLM business system. So, if you are working to recruit people, it is advised to expect more rejections than people signing up.

The same goes if you are working in an internet MLM. It is as hard convincing online people to follow and join you in your business. If you don't know how to generate leads, it is going to be more difficult for you to accumulate members.

In fact, the fastest way to make that internet MLM work out is to have a generous and steady flow of MLM leads. Without a steady list of prospects who will be your future team members, your business will have a slim chance of growing. Unless you have a constant source of recommendations or referrals, you need to work out to get on those good leads.

If you have no idea how, check the following ideas.

Create a website

With a website, you will have a source where you can set up your own contact form which people can use to submit their personal information and email addresses. Be sure to build a great site so that more people will be interested visit and come back and you will rapidly earn a good sized mailing list.

Set up a Contest in your Site

A contest can be run in your website wherein participants are required to submit their entries complete with their contact information. You can offer prizes and in exchange you get their contacts so that you can promote to them your product or service.

Create a Social Network Account

This is another good way of accumulating a list of potential sales dealers for you. Nowadays, there are various social network sites that are free to sign up. Through these sites, you can earn prospects by inviting them to become your social network friends. Be sure to be nice always and avoid appearing pushy to avoid scaring them off.

Give Free E-books

Offering anything that is free is probably the easiest way to entice your readers to submit their email address and personal information. The free e-book can be sent out to every reader who agreed to receive the free item in exchange of entering their contact details and putting those in the mailing list. The one-time expense you spend on the free e-book is nothing compared to how much contact lists you are going to earn at the end of this scheme.

Multi Level Marketing Issues and Scams

In these days when all kinds of scams are affecting many people, it is no surprise that the successful multi level marketing (MLM) business concept is one that scam artists frequently copy. And unlike other business scams, MLM scams seem to be one of the most serious cases. The reason is that MLM scams, or better known as pyramid scams, often involve huge amount of money taken from each individual victim.

The worse thing about these scams is victims don't realize they were victims until the suspect or the company has disappeared from the scene without the slight warning. Sometimes, the scam is perfect enough that even the government fails to initially detect that there is something illegal into it such that the unscrupulous suspects get away fine with tons of robbed money in their pockets.

The sad thing about MLM scams is they have become a piece of the whole network marketing industry. Subsequently, if the person is not vigilant enough, they can get easily and lose their hard-earned money before they realize it. It is a given fact that because of the poor economy crisis, many are looking for the fastest way to double, and even triple, their money. As a result, more and more people fall trap to these scams.

Of course, the government is doing its part to protect the people by warning them how scams work and how to avoid them. For instance, giving out information that MLM scams are easily spotted when they don't have legitimate products or services to promote; when the people behind them look unreal; when their claims are too good to be true; and so on, and so on. So, at least, this information helps people to become aware of the existing scams and avoid being a part of them.

But, sometimes scams do not only happen on illegal companies. Sadly, some legitimate MLM companies do their own scam thing too albeit not in an illegal way.

See it this way. When people join a legitimate network marketing company, they are assembled to be trained and taught things they are supposed to do in order to succeed in the business. They are taught how to go on a list of their whole family or friends, contact them and make appointments, bring sales, and recruit as business partners.

True enough, these tasks work and they were able to build a kind of network. But after exhausting the list, where do they go now? This is no problem. The company will instruct them to go out and find other people to recruit into their teams. Sounds simple, but the whole matter is that it isn't, particularly if you are not the type of person who can easily bond with a stranger.

So, what is the problem with the training? What they don't realize is that a hundred percent of the supposed training was not given to the members leaving them hanging in the air after the initial part of the whole work is achieved. Or simply, the effective way of generating new leads or list of new recruits for the business is missed. And because of this missed part, some of the members do not know what to do. They end up frustrated and start considering other things to do instead of continuing the started MLM work.

It happens all the time in the industry. So, if you are an individual who considers joining multi level marketing business group, don't just look for signs of MLM or pyramid scams. Even if you end up with a legitimate MLM group, find out if a hundred percent training is given to the new members to ensure you know what to do from the start until the peak of achieving success.

Multi Level Marketing - The Right Way for Online Promotion

In contrast to what most MLM people believe, the online promotional campaign of any multi level marketing business differs from that of the offline scheme. Some of the campaign techniques that are basically applied to the offline MLM venture are not suited to the online campaign. Thus, you can't expect the same rate of success.

To set things straight, you must know one fact. The offline promotion follows the one-on-one approach whereas the online promotion is led by the one-on-many approach.

Understanding the Difference of both Approaches

Offline One-on-One Approach

When you conduct MLM offline, it is vital that you have a one-on-one discussion with a potential client. It may be a single individual or a group but what is very crucial is that you have a face-to-face meeting with a possible client. This chance allows you to touch on their emotions, to persuade them, and call them to action. You have a better hold of their need so you will know how to serve them better with your product. At the same rate, you can follow up on them. If they respond, then, presto! You get yourself a downline. When your potential client expresses disinterest, you can move on and talk to another target.

Ideally, online MLM campaign is more powerful. Instead of focusing on one individual or one specific group, the modern technological Internet tool lets you reach out to a larger number of people who are already enticed in MLM. These people are too willing to invest their money to promote the business. With this kind of potential clients, you can train them about how to go on with the MLM program in an instant. An online campaign likewise provides you with more leads in a wink of an eye. As a result, you grow a bigger down-line and earn more financial rewards.

Doing it Right

How do you go about with an online MLM business? Take a look at the insights below.

Promote the business through some online business ezine. Ezine is a term used to refer to the electronic publication that is sent out by the publishers on a regular basis. It is sent to the readers through email. The readers of the ezines are those who have fair interest in business topics so they are likely to be motivated to pay attention to your MLM business and partake in its promotion. You can have your ads in the ezine for a specific fee.

Use pay-per-click search engines. As a powerful method, pay-per-click hosts to several successful online MLM businesses. You pay a certain fee for every "click" in your website. If you make use of this method, your own MLM promotional campaign ad will show up on the search result page especially if someone keys in the MLM-related keywords.

Promote through the paid safe lists. This method sends your promotional campaign directly to the eager individuals who actually prefer to read all your ads. The paid safe list's readers are able to receive more ads compared to those who receive the e-zines.

Use short, recognizable and easy to memorize URLs. It will help a lot if your potential customers are able to memorize your URL in case that they want to visit your website once more. When they sign up under you, you will serve as their upline.

Online multi level marketing can be challenging but that is its very nature as a kind of business. Keep these tips in mind and you will surely find a great spot online for your MLM business.

Factors To Consider When Searching For The Greatest MLM Opportunities

Multi level marketing (MLM) may likewise be a new term for you. To give you a general idea, the term means that a certain recruitment procedure is involved to convince someone to become a part of a certain networking team. The said team will be working to gain sales.

As a member of an online MLM promotional campaign, you should try your best to distribute or sell the products electronically or by means of referring some potential clients to a certain affiliate website. If you are connected with an offline MLM business, then, you have to conduct the one-on-one approach wherein you have to meet with a potential client, talk, and convince him or her to avail of your product. It is actually simpler said than done. In truth, there are a lot of things that you have to learn if you want to become successful in any MLM opportunity that you venture in.

It is crazy to think that because MLM is a networking business, you can just sit back, relax and earn your money even with the slightest effort. It is a wrong notion. Even when you are the up-line of several other people, you can't simply depend on them to sell and distribute the products. You have to constantly follow up on them, enhance their selling skills, give them the right training, and monitor their performance. All of you work as a team so it is necessary that you do your best and exert the right amount of effort to facilitate the growth and progress of the business.

You probably have one goal if you are a newbie in the network marketing industry or you are currently an active member of it. That is, to have a taste of success so you will feel that everything that you are doing is worth it. With the myriad of information circulating both online and offline, you may already be confused as to which opportunity should you grab.

If you feel this way, it is best to consider the following criteria so that you will not go wrong with your choice of an MLM opportunity:

The company's reputation: A lot of networking companies exist and they are too insistent on signing you up as a member. Take note that you must only get attached to one company that has a credible reputation as led by a sensible leader. The company should be governed by a purposeful mission and vision that is not only going to work for its own benefit but yours as well.

The training: Don't hesitate to inquire. You can ask some people in the company or some members of the downline and see how they are doing and benefiting from the promised compensation. You should know the kind of support system that you will be getting should you join the company.

Personal link with the product or service: It is impossible for you to endorse a product or a service that you don't personally believe in. The trust on the product or service must start within yourself because such feeling will motivate you to enthusiastically promote it.

The compensation package: Be sure that you inquire regarding the pros and cons of the promised compensation package.

These factors are very crucial in identifying your success in doing business with any multi level marketing company. With the right judgment, decision, and insight, your success is certain to materialize.

How To Deal With Multi Level Marketing Advertising

It is natural to feel overwhelmed whenever you have any sort of business venture. You get excited, enthusiastic, and very energetic. This normally happens as you have registered for a multi level marketing opportunity. However, there comes the time that all the excitement and other overwhelming emotions die down. You are faced with the realization that the moment to get started has come. The question is, how do you get on with an MLM business? What are the elements and factors to consider in achieving success?

First Things First

Before you count your blessings, you must first come up with a solid plan on how you must get on with an MLM business. Plan your steps. Know the requirements. Come up with specific scripts that will grab potential clients' attention and motivate them to make a decision. Another factor that you should focus on is the advertising concerns of your MLM business.

Some MLM people commit the mistake of incorporating the wrong steps in advertising their products or services. Don't make the same faults if you don't want to fail in this endeavor. Take a look at the following tips to boost your own MLM advertising.

Tip #1. Refrain from using the name of your company or specifying your product in your advertising campaign. There are a lot of MLM firms that forbid their affiliates from using their names in the course of advertising. You have to believe it but it actually brings forth a good effect.

Tip #2. Focus on your goal. Your main goal is not about brand awareness. Your main concern is to build target leads, grab their attention, and let them take the opportunity. Your bottom line is to emphasize briefly what your product and service can generally do to benefit them.

Tip #3. Don't give too much information. Tease them so that they will contact you for further information. Don't ever spoil the magic and appeal of advertising.

Reasons Why You should be Careful with Income Opportunity Advertisements

Generally, MLM companies that deal with income generating opportunities want to be very careful and discreet when it comes to their ads. There are a few vital reasons and they are:

Credibility. When you advertise an income opportunity but the company itself is not doing well, then the issue on credibility arises. This lessens the chances of people joining your network.

Sustainability. This is yet another issue to settle especially when your members are those who are only after the financial gain. They are likely to stick with you because they want their pay checks. The secret to MLM success is the bondage that attaches the members to the products and their commitment to facilitate the growth of the business.

Notice-ability. There are hundreds of MLM companies out there to do business. You should offer something special. Mention it in your ads. Be sure that your announcement is catchy and is sure to stand out.

Advertising medium. Where should you place your ads? There are numerous mediums to use. You may opt for the newspapers, trade journals, pay-per-click, blogs, direct mail, email, radio, web 2.0, post cards, newsletters, and many more.

The way you design your multi level marketing advertisements determine the leads that you may gather and eventually the monetary reward that you will enjoy in the future. Hence, take note of these important tips!

How To Meet Multi Level Marketing Success

Can you actually meet success in multi level marketing without even trying? The answer is NO. Some people will make you believe that MLM is a kind of business that doesn't require any effort on your part. Well, those who fall for this false belief is indeed a fool.

It is largely in contrast with what other MLM people tell you that with your downline working, there is nothing left for you to do other than wait and claim for financial rewards. In reality, you have to try your best, devote your time and effort, and even invest your own money if you want to succeed in any MLM business venture of yours.

Is MLM really difficult?

Just like any other business, doing MLM is quite challenging. After all, you have to invest time, money, and effort on it. The main reason on why some people feel that it is too tough is because they lack the right knowledge on how to build and maintain the network as well as to run the business itself.

What are some of the wrong reasons on why MLM businesses fail?

One of the main reasons is because some MLM people make use of the "inbound" type of recruiting method. Several individuals are mistaken because what they typically do is to throw some information like the company's name and nature, the products being sold, and the compensation rewards. They give out these details as soon as they see individuals or groups that are worth talking to. Of course, when the compensation package sounds tempting, many folks are likely to join even when they don't really have a full grasp of what the task is all about.

Companies and MLM entrepreneurs think that the bigger the network is, the higher sales possible. They make the mistake of recruiting people because of sales purposes which is a very self-centered reason.

An "outbound" recruiting method is defined as the step in identifying the real prospects by looking into a certain phase in their lives. People who want something in their lives to change are the ones that you need in the business. Thus, recruiting is all about getting the people because they want to do it to change an unwanted condition in their lives and not because you want them to do something for you. It is a matter of considering their needs and wants and not just to focus on what you want and what you need.

Another reason on why MLM fails is due to recruiting the wrong people. It is important that those whom you sign up to partake in your business are the ones who want to solve an unwanted condition in their lives. It will motivate them to be dedicated and enthusiastic in making the sales grow for the better. So, if you simply accept everyone who signs up even those who are just there because of the fun or challenge that they may have, then, your business is not going to get its target success!

Hence, to meet multi level marketing success, you should partner with people who have a strong desire for change, people-oriented, have the ability to influence clients, active in the community and other business-related groups, and are financially gifted so they can boost the growth of the business.

Internet Multi Level Marketing Advantages

Multi level marketing (MLM) is a business concept that involves selling the products by encouraging other people to be in your team. A commission is earned from every product you sold as well as from the products the people in your down line (pyramid group) have sold. Obviously, if you have managed to create a big team, it will mean big financial rewards for you.

But what if it is a small team? Surely, you will never get to dramatic results from that, won't you? Such is a common problem with multi level marketing business. If the member is not bolder enough to encourage other people to become their down line, making it to huge financial success is a hard job.

But then, any business requires hard work to come to success. Even internet multi level marketing business needs hard work, though not as physically tedious as traditional MLM. But when you think how a typical MLM business works, the internet marketing makes it more advantageous to people who do not excel in verbal communications, let alone sales talking, with other people. In a traditional MLM scheme, you make use of guerilla marketing strategies in order to attract people to sign up under your down line. If you exhausted your list, you are required to deal with strangers in the name of recruiting new members. You have to give flyers and leaflets to people and entice them to get interested.

Limiting to one area would not give you high chances of getting them signed up under you. Still, you need to exhaust all means such as putting flyers or leaflets on other people's cars, leaving leaflets around where people can pick them up, billing leaflets to people's mail boxes, and similar techniques. But as tediously exhausting as it is, you are still faced with the challenge that not many of these people will even get a second look and be interested.

Some aren't just interested because they simply don't believe about the scheme while others may look at it as another typical scam trying to hook people with their money. Some are not interested because the typical MLM concept requires large money for the initial investment while others are just too busy to care about your flyers and leaflets.

So, from the hundreds of people who got the leaflets and flyers, you may probably have only a single phone call inquiring about your business. With luck, you can have that call turned into a sign-up member to your team. With more luck, that person will turn out to be a hard-working member that helps to make your team bigger. If not, better luck next time for you.

For the people who hate all the above work, the internet multi level marketing seems to be the ideal alternative. It does not require tedious physical work to convince people. There is no money used up to make and distribute those papers. There is no huge sum needed to bring the supply of physical products.

The internet MLM business has electronic products to be supplied. Referring or recruiting new members is done via the internet. Business deals are done online. Obviously, the internet has more advantages to people who don't have the guts to work outside home. So, if you want to be involved in a money-making scheme that brings real money to your bank but do not want to be doing all those hard work stuffs above, you can try the internet multi level marketing business.

If you want more information, you can research, again, the internet to find effective ways to use the methods correctly in order to be a success.

Key Secrets In Turning Multi Level Marketing Opportunities Into Rewards

If you have finally decided to actively join the network marketing industry, you know for a fact that things can be a lot different as compared to your traditional orientation. You should apply some techniques that will heighten your chances to earn more. Multi Level Marketing includes the process of recruiting people into a team so that everyone can work hand in hand to handle the sales and distribution of the products. The good news is that being the leader, you earn your commission whenever one of your members is able to make sales.

Being new to the MLM thing is likely to leave you dazed and confused. To help you sort things out, it is best to go through some simple yet powerful training. Of course, your up-line will be willing to help you out but there are times when you need to work by yourself. You can never depend on them at all times. Earning the monetary reward is a challenge that is posed to all of you who work for the team. You may belong to the same group but you still have that feeling of competing with the others.

Network marketing is but a personal game. You need to mark your own sales before you can receive any points. Thus, you must concentrate on learning the basic secrets that will boost your progress.

Among the skills that you have to learn and acquire are:

How you can inspire the people to join in your own network. You may be a member of an up-line but sad to say, there are several people ahead of you. You can also convince other people to become members of your down-line. All that you must do is to learn which buttons to push to motivate them.

How to mark potential clients who can help you succeed in your venture.

You should know how to determine the probability that a visitor can turn into a potential client. You must become an expert in discerning as to whether or not a person is going to do business with you.

How to coach your down-line so that they will be motivated to bring in new members?

If there are more members in your team, it means that as the leader, you have more chances of earning more whenever one of them sells the products. Thus, you should be willing to teach your members the secret of motivating people to sign up as affiliates.

How to consolidate your obligations as the leader.

You must master the art of being a team player. You are not only a leader but a member at the same time.

Hence, be sure that you know all your duties to let your MLM team succeed.

How to be creative to expand your existing group.

Again, there is a bunch of benefits for a bigger group.

How to grab an opportunity and make the best out of it.

There is a need to study a current opportunity and uncover ways on how you can turn such into a monetary advantage.

Multi Level Marketing will seem to be a tedious task for someone who doesn't take time to uncover its very nature. Hence, if you are truly serious about being in the network marketing business, it is a must for you to learn these secrets.

Making Money Out Of Multi-Level Marketing

If you are someone who likes to try everything in the name of increasing monetary compensations, most likely, you have been into multi-level marketing. If you are a success with it, that is certainly good news. If you are just starting and finding it hard to do it the right way, this article is perfect for you. Check the following information to learn more about the legitimate way of doing multi level marketing.

Who Are the Best Candidates?

Multi level marketing is most ideal to the people who want to do business, own their time, and make their pay-check without producing their own merchandise or product. It is better suited to people who possess excellent leadership skills, hard work, and commitment to promote and sell products. And it is even best suited to people who, even though do not basically know how to promote and sell products, have the ability to create pyramid-like group – meaning to recruit new members to sign up with the company and be one in the down lines.

One advantage of this marketing strategy is that members do not necessarily have to worry because business and marketing plans are always provided. All they have to ensure is to follow the guidelines and directions stated in the plans. Further enhancement of the strategy can be applied as long as it does not create problems with the existing one.

Choose the Company Properly

It is a fact that multi level marketing scheme has always been associated with illegal pyramid scams. It is in this note why prospective clients have to be always vigilant when intending to join any multi level marketing team. Choosing companies that have good reputation of developing people is a smart way of starting it. Most multi level marketing companies focus in sales while others do not even engage their members in developing their own marketing strategies. Good MLM companies do not simply concentrate on numbers. They make good leaders out of their own members.

It is also a wise move if you work with top marketers or top earners. You will be able to work with reputable and established companies or corporations, which have already eliminated much of the known hassles associated with this marketing scheme; therefore, you are assured of guaranteed success as long as you are in the right direction. These top networkers provide regular conferences to educate members of relevant marketing strategies so that they continue to learn effective ways to be a success in this field.

As you join a network group, it is imperative that you choose an up line which supports all its down line members. The up line member should administer field coaching and reinforce sales and managing skills of the down line members. A good network company must also provide free custom website where members could use it as their training online site and to motivate them to action as well as bond with the other teams.

Do A Lot of Research Before Joining

As illegal pyramid schemes have become rampant nowadays, it has become tricky what is the legitimate strategy or not being offered by the multi level marketing company. As a result, many have become unfortunate victims who have invested money in which never returned. In these days when it is becoming difficult to trust business teams, it is therefore vital that you investigate a lot before dropping any amount of money in hope to invest and make profits out of it.

There are many avenues where to get information about legitimate multi level marketing companies and making sure you go to these sources will at least avoid you from being a victim too.

Multi-Level Marketing Commissions

If you are frequently short with money at the end of the month, joining a business that requires you to sell product is one good option. You earn commission from the sales you make, and the more products disposed the larger income you will get. But the problem with this kind of business marketing is, unlike in multi level marketing business, earning substantial amount of money is not possible for the most dealers, especially those who are in the lower levels.

The reason is products pass through a number of distributors that by the time commissions are to be paid, there are many who need to share the income sales. In business methods like this, the products that come from the manufacturer have to go to the warehouse distributor and then to the area distributors.

They would eventually go to the sub-distributors who will pass them to the dealers and finally to the retailers. The retailers buy the products from the higher level, which in return, buys their stock from their upper level, and so on.

In this type of business, the emphasis is always put on selling. Each level has to fill an order and replenish an inventory by purchasing the products from the next upper level. If the sub-distributors of the distributor did not sell enough products, the distributor still has to purchase stocks from their higher level in order to keep their distributor's status – otherwise, they would lose it. So, even if there are still products in the inventory, the distributor needs to use money from their own pocket to buy stocks for their future sales.

The Multi Level Marketing Experience

The multi level marketing business concept was taken from the above marketing method. However, the emphasis was not on selling products but more on recruiting sales people. It was more than 50 years ago when the first multi level marketing strategy was launched where the products used were nutritional supplements.

Contrary to the other method of selling products, the companies that used multi level marketing concept do not need a number of distributors and retailers in order to dispose them. Instead, they only need their members to take the products which were acquired from the manufacturers and let them distribute directly to the market.

The main goal of this business model is to have more and more people to join and each of them make their purchase. Why is this so? Each member to sign up with the company needs to buy the product. Logically, if 100 members would sign up, there are 100 sales. If 10,000 members were recruited, 10,000 sales would be achieved; thus, more income for the MLM business team.

The Commission

Whether the member sells anything or not, they still have income from a commission earned from every member recruited. In order to make the sales, all recruited members are required to buy a certain amount of product. In most cases, the amount of the product is already included in the signing-up fee. Each month, the members need to buy the product in order to qualify for the commission from their recruited dealers.

There are levels in which the newly recruited members have the option to choose from. The higher level they buy or sign up with, the higher commission fees they would get. They also have the option to earn the commissions without buying enough amount of product by recruiting enough number of dealers of members each month.

Multi Level Marketing And How It Boosts Internet Marketing

Multi Level Marketing or MLM is recognized by many experts as an effective way to sell and market the products by means of recruiting a network of people to be under your team. Through which, you get your commission not only by selling the products by yourself but also when any of the members of your team successfully sell something. This goes to show how financially rewarding it can be for you if you happen to manage a big team.

So, are you up for the challenge? Are you ready to earn more money and hit the Internet marketing industry?

The Internet Industry as a Fast Money-Making Scheme

There is no doubt that any business conducted over the Internet has higher probabilities of becoming successful. For one, the Internet is the portal that reaches out to potential customers all over the world. Second, any business done online works and sells faster.

Overall, Internet marketing is obviously filled with advantages. It is not only the number one mode of doing business but is likewise a rewarding experience for anyone who decides to try it out. The operation may be really tedious since you have to be active 24/7 but you are likely to jump for joy if you think of the rewards that you may get out of it. You should have an email auto responder and several other facilities that work towards getting back to the customers in no time.

How to Recruit People into Your Team

Generally, the guerrilla marketing techniques are employed in recruiting people into the team. Although the business target is done online, you still need to get in touch with live people who will be willing to be in the same team with you. An old school technique that you can follow is that of distributing some flyers and leaflets on the streets, leaving them in cars, stuffing them into the mailboxes, and the likes. Similar methods like these are known to work provided that you include your contact details. Those who are interested may contact you and then work for you.

You don't have to dwell into the abyss of hopelessness. For at least one hundred distributed leaflets, you are to get at least 10 phone calls from individuals who stand interested on the opportunity that you are providing them with. Success is more likely to come your way even with a smaller group to start with. With too much perseverance and hard work, your financial gains will be within reach.

The Secret to the Success of Internet Marketing

You probably know how hard it is to convince people to sign up and be recruited. At first, their minds are clouded with doubts. Is this a scam? Is there a bit of truth in what this flyer indicates? To convince them to become members of your multi level marketing team means an extra effort on your part. You don't have to use any further flowery words to make them change their minds. You just have to tell them straight what they can get out of their efforts. The power of words comes in here!

Now, Internet marketing allows you to earn more at such a short time. You should incorporate the tried and tested methods. It is by getting involved in an online multi level marketing that you simply deliver the products electronically and refer the possible clients to the affiliate websites! It is easy, right?

Multi Level Marketing: How to Avoid The Scams

Multi level marketing (MLM) is a business strategy formed fifty years ago, and ever since, has become popular that until now certain business groups use to enhance their productivity and success rate. But this form of marketing strategy did not escape the critical eyes of the many observers, who questioned its validity and capability to really bring more people good amount of money. Despite these controversies, there are multi level marketing companies which have been above success rates and have been allowing other people to share the monetary benefits.

Perhaps, it is due to the fact that these successful companies did not stop discovering new ways to enhance their strategy business models instead of sticking to an outdated scheme. While there were stories of scams leading people to doubt multi level marketing, successful companies did see the need to update MLM strategies to tailor-fit the ever changing trend of the burgeoning technology. As a result, the applied network marketing plans gave them high financial rewards that other archaic marketing business concepts never made possible.

As expected, the success of multi level marketing was used by scam groups for their own benefits. Pyramid scams, which resembled the networking marketing business structure, started to come out to mislead people and rob them of their own money. Because of this, it is more important than ever that you know exactly what it involves when joining a multi level marketing team.

The most important thing to remember when joining is to distinguish legitimate multi level marketing groups from pyramid scams.

It is easy. Unlike legitimate multi level marketing groups, pyramid scams strategize by offering the same structure but without any product or company to endorse them. Illegal pyramid scams offer a business marketing set-up, which is meant to entirely fool the prospective clients until the poor victims invest a certain amount of money. After recruiting members and pocketing all their money, the company suddenly disappears and then moves on to hook victim prospects using another scam plan.

If you want to avoid them, there are ways to find those legitimate multi level marketing companies.

1.) Do your assignment by making a background check to any company you are about to join. It should have a physical address, contact numbers (telephone numbers), and a website. Make sure it is legally listed and has been operating or in existence for a long time. Be sure to know who the legitimate owners of such company. Check backgrounds of the names referred to you as scam artists can easily use them although were actually not affiliated with the company.

2.) A good sign that the company is legitimate is there are products existing. Even so, be sure that you checked these products and where do they come from. Find out if the company develops and owns the products and if they have them in abundant supply. Be aware that some scam artists may present products but in reality, do not have them in large supplies.

3.) Another way to find out if the company is operating a legitimate multi level marketing business structures is how big the operation is going on. Large companies may operate their business through the whole nation, abroad, and even worldwide. Always be skeptical if the company is small. Though they do not necessarily be scams, it is often a good idea to always check on the operation to make sure you don't end up with a fraud.

Multi Level Marketing: A Brilliant And Legitimate Concept

Multi level marketing or MLM, despite its success for the past half a century, has gained the most horrible reputation in the industry. The criticism went on and on until the remarkable business concept has come to the point where almost everybody is scared to be part of it. Whenever one hears the word MLM, it is almost instantly that people think of it as scam, pyramid rip-off, and other worse terms. But the thing is, it has been a successful business scheme ever since.

For the past 50 years, many companies have benefited from its advantages while more and more are beginning to use the concept for their business plans. So, despite the horrible reputation, what makes these companies continue to use such method for bringing more sales to their products/services?

Simple. It works! How can it work for you? Again, very simple!

1.) The first thing to do is to look for a legitimate company with a product or service that you desire to be connected with. While considered the simplest, it is the most vital initial step.

2.) Next task is to create a network by recruiting members who will distribute your product/service. Commissions are earned from direct product sales and from royalties earned from direct sales of your network.

3.) And then, keep recruiting and encouraging the down line to recruit more members so the team gets bigger. The bigger the team, the high monetary rewards for everyone.

It is different from the typical way of marketing, where a lot of time is spent before the product gets to the buyers and the pay gets to the worker. In the MLM business, those players in the field are removed from the scene so that it is only you and the manufacturer that is involved. The product gets promoted only by word of mouth, so unnecessary expenses from ads are removed from that too.

As a result? Instead of paying many people, you are the ones who get paid from the commissions earned from your MLM team's sales. That's the reason why MLM companies can afford paying hefty sums to the members. Clearly, the one who started this marketing concept 50 years ago is such a remarkable, brilliant business maker.

If you are still afraid at the mention of MLM or multi level marketing, here is another viable reason why you should look at this concept in a different light. It is often that products are made with superior class and quality so that what the consumers, or actually the members, will get are only worthy of their money. Because it has become hard for the people to convince or entice other people to trust how MLM works, it is more important than ever that manufacturers come up with only a product that people will find useful and worth every cent spent.

So, why should you dismiss the horrible belief about MLM business? It is because the method is a very amazing business plan that works. It is a business that doesn't require you to spend hundreds of thousands of dollars to start. And it is the most ideal choice for people who can't stand working in a nine to five job.

Don't get caught up in your fear about multi level marketing. What you should do is to get a second glance and see what it really has to give you. It is not too late to reap that financial rewards you so long all these years.

Multi Level Marketing Business - Tips To Start With

As you have decided to join a multi level marketing (MLM) business, you will feel a bit relaxed for a few days up to a month. If you are a member of a downline, then, most probably your upline will be very much willing to help you. Now if you are the leader of the team, then, for sure you are obligated to work on your leads. This holds true for people who normally want to earn more and set good examples for those in their downlines.

Apart from busying yourself in finding the perfect leads, you also need some other secrets to keep your MLM business running. This article is going to lead you to some secret ingredients in the success of every MLM business entrepreneur.

Empower Your Business

The success in any form of business doesn't come overnight. You have to work hard for it. MLM is also known as the networking business. It includes the process of recruiting people who will be willing to sign up and be in your team. As you get yourself involved in pyramiding, it is your duty to look for members, train them, and of course sell products so you can earn money. Being on top of the pyramid allows you to earn whenever any of the people in your down-line closes a deal.

The real secret to it is that of providing some good training background for everyone in your team. They make a sale and you earn too!

Vital Business Tips

Determine the company's stability. This is a prime concern especially if you are new in the business. There are several networking companies out there who offer you partnership but don't trust them too much. Find out if the company has been in operation for a number of years already and know its status as well as its credibility.

Find out your own availability. Are you willing to put much of your time and effort in this kind of business? Take note that networking business includes recruiting people, training them, and selling products.

Find out if there is enough reason to believe in the product that you are selling. You can't practically sell something that you don't believe in. If you don't, then, what is the chance of your team members to believe in it? Your own belief will determine your enthusiasm to sell it.

Ascertain your confidence about the business. If you are confident that your business is important in each person's life, then, most probably you will be happy to tell your relatives and friends about it.

Determine the helpful tools. Many of the MLM networking companies provide their members with the helpful business tools. Find out if your company will make it available too.

Find out how the company website targets to meet the needs of the customers. An online website is one proof of the legal existence of a company. However, it doesn't end in it. The website should make available a support system that will help generate leads.

Whether you are going to work full-time or part-time for a multi level marketing business, it is necessary that you take note and integrate these vital business tips. After all, success only comes to those who work hard for their own business ventures.

Multi Level Marketing: The Cheap And Fast Selling Method

To boost sales of the company's products, marketers are constantly on the lookout for good business system. If you would observe it, the traditional marketing systems have left an impression that they were having signs of stagnating.

Except for some who have made a phenomenal foundation in the business world, selling products have become pretty difficult nowadays. This is because of the many competitive companies trying to outsell each other. Even the leading brand companies were facing the dilemma of increased sales commissions from the retail chains and distributors.

Because of the faced tough competition, market researchers are convinced that the multi level marketing, or simply MLM, is one marketing strategy that is currently an effective method of generating product sales of today. Now, manufacturers and companies have seen a way to raise their hopes high once more.

Unlike the other conventional business method, the MLM is a cheap and fast way of selling products. This is because the sales agents are direct marketers of the company. They form a network wherein each member is required to buy a minimum amount of the product.

Let's say the network consists of 100 members. Logically, there are going to be 100 sales from that network. And from the sales made to this network alone, the company is already assured of good turnout. And what if the network consists of 10,000 members? Additionally, what if most of the members of the network buy more of the product?

- Obviously, profits are going to flow substantially from the sales made by the members of the network.

So, what about the profits for the sales agents, who come from the network structure?

- For every recruit of the member, a guaranteed sale is targeted since all network members are required to buy a certain amount of product from the company. For each recruited member, the marketer at the higher level earns commission from them. Now, if the member has recruited many members, it is rational to assume that there is going to be large commission or income from that.

Accordingly, the main core of the multi level marketing method is primarily not on the selling but on the recruiting ability of the people.

Generation of Leads

The problem of most people with MLM method is their incapability to build their own network of members. As they exhaust their potential lists of future sales leaders, they no longer know what to do until they become inactive such that sales of products begun waning as well as flow of income slowing down.

Now, this is where generation of leads comes into play. As the companies do not want to stop the success they got from using MLM business method, the marketing specialists introduced a new system to the method, which is the generating of leads.

The leads are created from the people who were already screened and have expressed interest in joining the MLM business team. The screening process includes testing their commitment and skills. It takes time to create leads, but if you want to yield endless list of potential future sales leaders, it is a good way to go.

Generating leads in a traditional multi level marketing business system requires you to go out and hold the screening process in all major cities and towns. If you have extra budget, hiring a lead generation specialist company to do it for you is another good solution.

Either way, both are viable options to build a robust network team for you.

Multi Level Marketing Techniques To Get The Leads

What if you have already done your best and totally exhausted your leads that you know of? What should comprise your list now? What are you supposed to do? What would happen to your multi level marketing (MLM) business?

You might be wondering how some successful MLM business entrepreneurs manage to get their leads. Believe it, they make use of the tried and tested techniques! Anyone who is involved in the MLM industry should know the right approach. Take a look at the techniques below and apply them in your very own business.

Put up a powerful content. It helps a lot to open an online portal. A website about your business can be more helpful if you feature not only your products but other marketing tips, business opportunities, free tools, free articles, and any other information that talks about what the needs of potential visitors. When you do so, more people will be engaged to visit your website and you can increase the chances of convincing them to avail of your products as well.

Dangle the carrot. As soon as some visitors have been engrossed to reading what you have as a free content, be sure to get hold of their information. This will give you the opportunity to follow up on them and eventually offer them your products. The carrot here refers to a special but free report about email marketing, an e-book on how to create and manage a website, a newsletter, or an e-course that is basically designed to answer their needs on how to start their dream business. Just be certain that what you are going to send them as freebies are directly related to what they originally searched for in your website. When you have their contact details, you already have your leads!

Offer a special email course. You can become an MLM expert in an instant by offering potential clients an email course. You can do this through multiple auto responders. You can always get a copywriter if you think that you can't write things on your own. Include your business, products, and other opportunities being offered at the end for a more powerful final salvo.

Be sure to rank high. The pay-per-click search engines can help you in this endeavor. Be particular with the keywords and key phrases to use so that your website will be search-able. Also, employ a valuable and convincing content and newsletter that can heighten your sales.

Buy leads. You can buy a leads list but it can be very expensive. However, you can be assured that your investment will be rewarded if you are certain that your lead source is really the best one. If it is the other way around, then most probably, you are just going to waste your money for nothing.

Establish a name in the industry. There are always perfect moments to discuss your business to the right people. If you happen to talk things to some individuals who care less, then most probably they will end up annoyed at you. Always sound like an expert. It is when you pique the interest of the right people that they will surely come to you and avail of your offer. You can likewise join forums and chat rooms wherein you may find those who are fairly interested.

Multi level marketing business progresses only when you have the perfect leads. Thus, know which technique should work best for you!

Quick Tips When Joining A Multi-Level Marketing Company

Because of the increasing number of pyramid scams, there are many people who exhibit doubts when it comes to joining multi level marketing business groups. But if you are determined to follow the success of other people in this field, you don't have to be scared as there are actually legitimate MLM companies out there and you just need to know how to distinguish them from scams by doing a lot of research. As for the reasons why you should join a legitimate MLM company, monetary success is always obviously the major motivation among the people who dream of becoming a multi level marketing success.

But though monetary is the leading motivator of the game, it is wrong to think or believe that multi level marketing business can give you instant wealth or overnight success. So, finding the fastest way to build wealth online is the first mistake that most people do; therefore, giving them one hindrance to actually be in their dream status in life. Any company you might stumble in the internet with anomalous claim of getting instant rich scheme by investing big amount of money will put your effort, and money, to shame.

In reality, any business never gets successful in a very short time. Logically, a multi level marketing business concept sounds really good if you change your psychology of thinking that it wouldn't give you wealth within minutes. The simple truth is that network marketing, whether online of offline, needs time to build you wealth just as any other archaic business models do. Therefore, be sure to manage your expectations and develop proper attitude before joining any multi level marketing company.

What to do to be a Success

Due to the economic crisis, many people are looking for ways to find success with a multi level marketing or MLM online. But if you are just starting it out, you may find it hard where to begin to pick the right ideas and proper information. If it is becoming tough on you, here are some tips to help you find your success with your dream.

Develop the Right Outlook

Just like in any endeavour, it is as always important to develop the right outlook to fuel success. This will help you avoid you from quitting as it gets you to strive no matter is the outcome of your efforts. The right outlook or mindset will always propel you to say yes and move forward even after failing to recognize success until you get one.

Find that Passion to Success

Having a passion to what you really want in life is another key to going on and eventually finding the right MLM business plan for you. Multi level marketing companies do promote products, so it is a good thing to find what products do your passion comes in so that you will actually enjoy what you are going to market to achieve monetary success. In the online world, there is much information you will come about so be sure to research everything before plunging into the business world.

Be Consistent

Consistency helps you achieve your success. When choosing for a promotional method or product, be sure that it is what you want and you know you will continue working with on a daily basis. Choosing something because you see it is the easiest and then changing to another because it didn't work out well with you afterwards is no good way to begin achieving the success that you want.

Solve That Multi-Level Marketing Dilemma

Someone who is interested in joining the multi level marketing (MLM) industry is going to do everything to learn the ropes of the trade. Perhaps you have gone to the extent of listening to recorded telemarketing calls and audio tapes, attending company training, reading e-books, sending out business cards, and then learning everything in the website that your partner company has provided for you. You have invested money but unfortunately, you are unable to see the rewards.

Understanding the Requirements

Partaking in an MLM business venture requires you to be motivated, excited, enthusiastic, committed, dedicated, and above all - to be positive. The rewards of your investment are not going to be visible in a span of a week. A lot of MLM investors suffer from the same ordeal. You should never lose hope.

Now if you happen to notice it, those who succeed in this kind of business are armed with the following vital points:

Excellent communication skills. You must do the talking! Communicating with the customers is not only done orally but also through the means of written communication. Not all people are gifted with the excellent communication skills so not all of them succeed in convincing and motivating the customers. You should harness your own skills for a guaranteed victory.

Hard work. Business-minded individuals usually have to sacrifice some things. A lot of them spend little time in sleeping. If you can't keep yourself awake and moving, then you have lesser potentials of maneuvering your business.

Capital. It is indeed hard to be involved in a business venture without the cash fund. Many of the entrepreneurs have money to start with. Thus, you should realize its importance.

Love for selling. Being a passionate salesperson makes a good businessman. You should be open to the criticisms and rejections that naturally come around in any field of business. You should never lose hope because it is normal to face challenges.

Understanding the Essence of Leads

Who are your leads? Of course, you may start with your friends and family members. The problem is that these leads don't last a lifetime. You will surely run out of leads and they will get tired of purchasing your products. Certainly, realization will finally dawn on you that you need to find more leads outside your circle. Or else, it means the death of your business!

The leads are your potential customers. There is no business that survives without any leads. Simply put, they are the life and blood of your business. Your success largely depends on how big your number of leads is. When you don't have them, who will buy your products? Who will let money in?

In the MLM business, it is important that you know how to get to your leads. You can send emails, place phone calls, join forums and chat rooms, buy a leads list, or send newsletters. There are businessmen who have been in the business for so long a time that the leads are actually the ones who come to them. However, for a starter like you, things are a bit different. You have to do the hard work.

One more thing, even with an automated system that can reach out to potential customers, it is necessary to establish personal relationships with both your clients and your networking members. It is by means of a personal relationship that a longer multi level marketing business attachment is built.

The Turning Point Towards Multi Level Marketing Success

How do you really get started with a multi level marketing business? Are you going to print out hundreds of brochures, flyers, and business cards? Should you distribute them to the people you see down the street? Who are going to be your leads? This article will tell you the efficient way of maneuvering your MLM business venture towards success.

The New Approach

You don't have to go through the same old school approach of printing out flyers, brochures, or business cards. You are not involving yourself in this kind of business just to stay out in the sun to hand those papers to the passersby. Actually, you can do better than that. Yes, this new and modern approach doesn't entail you to go out of your home. You can do the marketing without all the unnecessary fuss. All that you need is a reliable computer and a telephone! These systems can be copied by your downline without costing them too much.

Forget about those data capture sites, broadcast dialers, and a lot of other tools that some MLM people tell you of. They can't possibly work without your knowledge of how to get on with things. The first thing that you must learn is to enhance your own marketing skill. If you master everything, then, the rest follows.

The following are the steps that you can keep in mind:

Step #1. Develop your own expertise. You can't be an effective MLM person if you know nothing about the current market, its trend, and your product or service. Say for example, you are marketing a weight loss pill. It is vital that you educate yourself about calories, dieting, fitness, and the likes. You can achieve the appropriate knowledge by reading books, manuals, and magazines, doing your own research, joining fitness forums, or undergoing some formal training.

Step #2. Design your prospecting and closing scripts. How should you approach your clients? What are you going to tell them? MLM success largely depends on an effective and affective prospecting script. The closing script should be enticing and motivating that calls your potential client to action.

Step #3. Research for your leads. Apart from your family and friends, you need to search for other leads. The best thing to do is to buy a leads' list from a reliable source. They are the people who are willing enough to avail of your products. As you get hold of their contact details, you may start calling them, emailing them, sending them newsletters, and the likes.

Step #4. Test your script. You can try if you can get invites by calling people from your list. Don't leave messages on the answering machines. You should be able to talk to the person himself to deliver your piece.

Step #5. Set a quota of invites. You should be able to achieve a certain number of invites within the day. Tracking your progress will let you know how well your business is performing.

Step #6. Train your down-line. Each of the members in your down-line must have the courage and ability to talk to people. You can help them improve in their craft by coaching them with these steps.

Multi level marketing can truly be challenging. That is why; everyone involved must be willing to learn and willing to do his or her best.

Important Multi-Level Marketing Websites

Top 25 MLM Marketing Companies
http://www.nexera.com/top25/

MLM Watch
http://www.mlmwatch.org/

FORBES on MLM in the wrong hands
http://www.forbes.com/sites/donaldfrazier/2012/10/31/multi-level-marketing-in-the-wrong-hands-ripe-for-abuse/

MLM Company Rankings
http://www.mlmrankings.com/

MLM Network Marketing Business Journal
http://www.nmbj.com/

DISCOVER THE ESSENTIALS OF
TIME MANAGEMENT

BY

WARREN BROWN

Importance of Time Management

When a person learns time management skills, it will help them to spend more time on more difficult tasks. Because of everyday time constraints, we need to learn how to make the most of our time with our work by doing more important tasks.

Time Management Effectiveness

We handle many different fields depending on what we do. There are many time management techniques that would prove useful for several fields of life. For example, a student can learn and practice time management by applying time management techniques when doing their homework or projects. Using time management techniques and practices can and will help to ensure the quality use of your time and the efficiency of the results that they produce.

Rather than working harder, we can work smarter so that we may realize how much time we can save when we use time management practices. But the success of these techniques largely depends on how you appropriately follow your schedule. A person can tremendously reduce their stress levels when following some time management techniques.

Having A "To Do" List

A basic aspect for effective time management is creating a "To do" list. This can help you cope and deal with the problem of losing time frequently. It is not advisable, however, to have several "To-do" list at once since it might lead to confusion. It is important that you place your list on a location that is easily visible for you. Hence, you will be able to consult the list right away on what your next task is supposed to be.

Prioritize

Another good method of time management is to handle daily tasks by prioritizing the more important tasks first. By doing this, you can then be able to separate the tasks that you need to do in accordance with their relevancy and significance. Then, you can deal with each tasks one at a time.

Saying "No"

A very effective time management skill is the ability to say "no" when other less important tasks and affairs are brought up to you and you have more important pending tasks. By learning how to turn them down, it reflects your commitment to follow your schedule and accomplish the task at hand. Once you have mastered how to effectively do this, you will save a lot of time in the future. Not only were you able to finish your tasks in time, but you've also opened more opportunities to accomplish more.

Time Will No Longer Be Your Enemy

Managing your time is important for several reasons. The most apparent reason is merely completing the job within the time frame you have alloted for it. It saves you from eating up the rest of the time needed for other useful tasks. For some, time is considered an enemy.

But getting yourself familiar with these time management techniques will enable you to enjoy your tasks as you do them, and quit worrying about time as a factor. After all, you cannot stop time from running; you have to keep up with it.

There might no be dramatic changes that comes with proper time management. However, it allows you to become more effective and productive as you continue to plan your days ahead.

Advantages of Time Management

Having a job can be a stressful activity. Most people lose a lot of time just trying to think about their job. Too often, your job consumes you that it becomes a part of your everyday life and you tend to lose priorities on other activities. However, all of these are due to improper management of time.

The problems

Without proper time management, you could be facing a lot of stress. You have to remember that productivity does not just mean doing several things. You need to create a balance in these activities and make sure each are properly done. When you have so many things to consider, you are very much likely going to fail in meeting your deadline or you can schedule more than one meeting at the same time. This could lead to lower efficiency and lots of time wasted. Although you might not lose your job in the process, you could easily forsake other aspects of your life.

The remedy

Time management can help prevent such events from happening. This is because you won't have to worry about things when you schedule your events properly. You get a lot of stress relief and a lot of time to prioritize your life.

However, successful time management is quite tricky. You have to incorporate a little self-discipline in order to set up your events properly.

You also have to be more flexible with your goals and priorities. These prerequisites are easy to attain. You just have to learn the basic concepts in order to set things in motion.

Proper time management creates a few of the most powerful advantages within and outside your job sphere. Since all these problems stem from stress, the main advantage of time management is the reduction of stress. You probably have experienced chasing deadlines or suddenly realizing that you set up two meetings on the same date. You can prevent such scenario from happening if you practice clear time management plan and a timetable for your activities.

By having a clear plan, you give yourself the chance to set up a great schedule that suits your planned activities both in and out of the job. Furthermore, you avoid compromising the most important aspect of all your activities: your health.

Another good thing about having a successful time management program is having a higher chance of completing everything on time. When you miss a deadline, you fall out of favor with your boss. This leads to additional pressure to complete other tasks and even to outdo your other officemates. This leads to a lot of unnecessary pressure that may cause you to extend your work outside the office just to keep up. It might even mean that you will bring your work to the dinner table.

And the worse that could happen, you get so stressed out that you pass on the stress to your family members. The sooner you complete your tasks, the more you free yourself of all the stress.

The best thing about time management is that you get the chance to live your life on a proper routine. Your working schedule is not swamped and so you can leave enough time for relaxing and having fun. And despite of your hectic schedule, never forget to take a break from time to time as it helps you become more productive.

Why is Time Management so Important?

Time management is a common problem faced by most of us. Oftentimes, when you are swarmed with multiple tasks at once, it becomes extremely difficult to identify which ones you must complete first. Too often, people eat up what is supposed to be their free time to be able to accomplish all pending tasks in time.

It takes a considerate amount of skill in order to manage your time properly. If you are one of these people, you are usually able to control your time efficiently that you can even finish tasks ahead of time.

Let's try to analyse the importance of Time management in different fields.

Time Management in School

Due to more freedom merited to college students, it can become quite challenging for new (freshman) students to cope with time management. The liberty to choose your own schedule readily creates a false notion that they can do whatever the want. On the other hand, it reflects one's priorities and how you are able to properly appropriate them into your schedule.

With lack of proper time management, a student will have trouble coping up with deadlines set by professors. Most students would tend to slack off during vacant hours that they end up accomplishing nothing.

If a student has prepared his or her own list of work for the day, he or she will be able to properly allocate the time spent for extra-curricular activities and assignments.

Time Management at work

When it comes to your job, proper usage of your time is more particular. This is because you are paid for the hours of service you render to the firm. Hence, companies will try to ensure that each hour you spend at the office is utilized effectively for work. Despite of this, employees still seek out ways to have a break.

If time is not properly managed, employees could easily eat up more time for their "breaks" than what is spent on actual work. Hence, the company ends up requiring the employee to do overtime work just to finish a project. If the overtime rendered is reflected on your pay-check, then it is good for you. But if not, then you reap the unpleasant effects of poor time management.

The Essence of Time Management

With the varying scenarios presented, it all comes down to one thing – proper time management. It allows you to achieve more in less time as compared to doing things without following a suitable system.

By properly allocating your time, you will be able to finish your tasks much faster. Also, you are able to avoid overlapping tasks that tend to slow you down.

How is efficiency linked to proper time management? Listing your intended work for the day is more than just there for reminder. Instead, they also remind you in terms of importance and urgency. When you make a list, it is important that you also create a time table for each corresponding task. This way, you are compelled to follow them in the time frame that was indicated to increase efficiency.

Aside from becoming more efficient, you also become more responsible when you learn how to properly manage your time. You can not only set your priorities, but also provide equal time for both work and leisure. Being responsible with your time will work effectively whether in school or work.

Probably the biggest benefit you can get from proper time management is that it improves the quality of your work. When you have ample time to work on a certain task, you will have enough time to determine any mistake and have enough time to correct or improve on it. When you are cramming, you do not have this luxury of revision and hence mostly settle for what you can accomplish under the allowed time frame.

To those who fail to manage their time well, most of them work under pressure or hours before the deadline. Hence, they do not get the chance to check the quality of their work.

These are just a few of the practical reasons why Time Management must be practiced by anyone who wants to become more effective in their field.

Effective Time Management Training

Most losses incurred by companies are due to a lack of sound time management program. Then, it leads to high levels of stress in the work force because employees are pressured and forced to extend working hours just to meet the company's quota. Indeed, there is a need to chase deadlines and attend double meetings.

However, there is a way to remedy all that. There is no overnight solution to this type of problem. What you need is a slow and steady approach until you have perfected your scheduling needs until you are able to work free of any time-related stress.

Why time management?

Time management is a very important aspect of any business. In fact, most time management procedures even entail stress management as these two usually goes hand in hand. You might notice that levels of stress drop when you do not have to deal with several meetings and deadlines. It also means that you will be able to live out your life outside of the business sphere. Hence, it creates a more positive and holistic outlook.

Stress is crucial because it can tend to make things more complicated. Productivity levels of employees are affected by their time management planning and workload. Hence, if you are able to manage your time properly, you can allow your employees to tend to stress relief activities. Aside from increasing their potential, it allows for a tighter bond amongst fellow employees and superiors. That is how it can impact team building factor.

What do you get out of training?

Any successful time management training program begins with setting up a workable timetable that you and your employees can work with. It comes in a very comprehensive package that allows both manager and employee to meet halfway.

Any company that undergoes training will have the capacity to teach employees how to manage time. This means that unnecessary distractions can be avoided. These efforts extend far beyond ensuring a thriving business but also considers one of the most important aspect in any venture, and that is your health.

This kind of training focuses on increasing the amount of control and focus the company has over its goals and methods. This means that when you allow improvements to go into the necessary sectors of your business, you are able to increase your efficiency. Therefore, this kind of training strengthens the employees' ability to assess the situation and pick out assignments that can help them increase productivity levels.

Delegation of tasks is also addressed in such training. This is because managers sometimes think that employees are better at handling manual activities such as photocopying and sending. However, managers need to know that delegation of tasks is a huge risk. Some tasks are better done by the manager rather than passing them down to subordinates. Aside from being time-efficient, it saves a lot of energy and allows for a more productive workplace.

The problem

One basic misconception about time management is that it allows no time for break or relaxation. In fact, when you properly manage your time, you get the exact opposite. It allows the individual more time to relax because he or she will be able to set aside time for work and other activities.

Hence, any problems encountered in the workplace does not carry over to your personal lives. Therefore, you have successfully kept your business and other aspects of your life separate, as they should be.

Experiential Learning on Time Management Skills

Most of us use the Internet to access tips and tricks for proper time management. While others purchase self-help books available in bookshops. Even if these tips are reliable, most of them are usually universal. Hence, the tips are too general and there is no guarantee that they will work for you.

You can learn how to properly manage your time through experience. Online tips and books may add up to your knowledge on how to properly manage time. However, nothing can replace hands-on experience. Here are a few instances where you can learn how to properly manage your time through experience.

Your Parents or Guardians are Away

When parents leave their kids at home for a certain time period, they learn to be more responsible in a shorter period of time. When left at home with responsibilities like washing the dishes, cleaning the house, and doing laundry will force them to work out the chores first. It also teaches them how to prioritize work over other less important activities, such as playing outside. Only when they have accomplished the tasks assigned to them are they allowed to play.

This kind of training also encourages the kids to experiment on ways to maximize their own time.

Your kids aren't the only one that will benefit from this kind of training. When kids become responsible enough with their own time in finishing up their chores, parents also save a lot of time. Kids can now lend their hand when it comes to doing chores at home, instead of you having to do it all.

Planning Big Events

Event Planning also gives a lot of good experience for you when it comes to managing your time well. Planning events need a lot of long term and short term plans that you can apply later on in your personal life. When planning an event, you have a lot of activities to consider and things to prepare. Therefore, you need to list down the activities that you must attend to for the day.

Having 2 commitments at the Same Day

Dividing your time to fulfill 2 commitments at the same day is a hard feat. It usually needs experience for you to masterfully do it. When you have 2 commitments a day, set up time tables and "to do" list for your activities on that day.

Having 2 commitments also teaches you to be versatile (with regards to schedule) on different situations. Sometimes you might need to give more time to appointments, so you have to create schedules that would be versatile enough to give time to Appointment A without jeopardizing Appointment B.

Entering in a Relationship

Entering into a relationship may be the best learning experience for you to properly manage your time. Relationships are all about 'long term' commitments. Meaning, you have to properly allocate your time within a day, in such a way that there is a time relegated to doing your usual activities and there is also a time for your significant other.

You have to adjust your time or schedule so that you will not undermine your partner or your personal life. This is not an easy task to do specially because there are a lot of variable things you have to consider when in a relationship. It makes you aware of all these variables and teaches you to learn how to compensate so you can maximize the limited time you have.

As the saying goes, it is through experience that we can learn from our mistakes and improve on them. Experience will teach you how to properly manage your time even if you won't read a single book or a tip over the internet.

Personal Time Management

Managers nowadays have difficulty trying to manage their time. They are swarmed with several tasks at once, therefore it is seemingly impossible to be able to complete everything on time. Oftentimes, the work tend to consume even ones' personal life instead of being limited to the work sphere.

To address the problem at hand, this is when personal time management plays an important role. When you are capable of managing your time well, you won't have trouble trying to meet last-minute deadlines or encounter double meetings.

Why Do People Have Poor Time Management?

Proper time management is an essential factor for success. You cannot tend to be complacent just because you have used what could be proven methods in dealing with smaller projects. If you have used certain methods on some projects, you cannot expect the achieve the same success rate with larger or different projects.

By doing this, you will notice some discrepancy in the result of the project you are working on. However, you can do something about it. More especially in terms of changing your scheduling habit and become more efficient.

The Different Aspects of Personal Time Management

Time management involves various aspects. Almost all managers recognize one or two but very few can recognize all of them. Keeping track of your activities goes beyond the basic managerial skills. It even goes beyond project planning and effective delegation.

With this kind of time management, you will be able to reduce and even eliminate wasted time. You will also be able to decide whether you can accept workloads or not. The best part is that you won't have to bring your business to your home anymore. Moreover, all you need is a little self-discipline to make things work.

With waste disposal, you only have to look at the various sources of waste. This will allow you to pinpoint non-work related activities. However, it doesn't mean you have to eliminate all breaks. You have to be able to choose what is more important. After all, time management is all about identifying priorities and working on them.

When you want a subordinate to do something, there is always the risk that it won't be done on time. To make sure that something is done on time, it is better to do it yourself. This increases the level of productivity as you know what to do and how to do it. Even the simple task of photocopying a memo and affixing your signature on them can lead to delays if the bureaucracy is too pronounced and if the subordinates slip up.

Another big problem is when you have to decide whether you have to help someone else with their job. This may be in line with your goal of creating a harmonious workplace. However, this leads to loss in time for your own work.

You have to consider how much time you need to devote for your work. Also, you need to recognize the additional work that you might agree to do for your officemate. This way, you can choose whether to accept or defer a call for help. Of course, you also have to look at the nature of the job. If it is on contrast to your own field, then it might take longer to finish.

Personal time management is easy. Identify and set up your priorities. This way, you can manage time successfully.

Free Time Management Tips

People have always valued the essence of time. However, only a few people have mastered the skill of properly allocating their time for their work. We see a lot of books in book shops claiming they have the secret to proper time management. But do we really have to pay just to understand the secret of proper time management?

You really don't have to buy these books to understand the secret of Proper Time Management. All you need is common sense and discipline. However, there are more reliable ways to achieve your goal. Here are a few tips to help you manage your time.

Before you go and start making a list of things you need to do, you have to realize that the list will never work if you won't back it up with discipline. When talking about discipline here, it means you have to know your own priorities as well to guide you in abiding with the rules that you have set for yourself.

1. List a set of things to do for the day – This is the traditional way to proper time management. Make a list of things you have to do for the day to keep you informed on what to do for the day. The list will help you to avoid distractions if any should arise during the day.

It is recommended to create a flexible "to do list"; having a flexible list allows you to fit unexpected events and occasions (only important ones) without destroying the whole list.

2. Change Bad Time Management Habits – It usually helps for starters to change their Bad Time Management Habits. If you reflect on your everyday activities, you'd probably realize that you spend a lot of time watching too much TV or other forms of leisure. It is okay to spend time on leisure, but never when it exceeds the allotted time for it. Changing these habits would increase your time to do more meaningful activities.

3. Set some things to do for the day as top priority. – The idea of setting hierarchies among your list of priorities is that those on top of the list are what you need to attend to first. It also helps you to finish on time when you use it in conjunction with your "to-do" list and daily timetable.

4. Learn how to say "NO" – When offered to do something, most people have trouble refusing. Hence, they are confronted with more tasks than they can manage. This is more important when it comes to tasks that are less important, such as watching a movie or going to a football game. You have to remember that once you have completed your pending tasks, you will have time to enjoy yourself.

If you're planning to go out, you have to plan this a few days ahead. Therefore, you can finish your task ahead as well to save enough time for these long breaks.

5. Dividing your workload – This is especially helpful when working with other people as a team. You don't have to do everything yourself. When you divide your workload, people tend to finish faster because they can focus on doing a specific task.

6. Keeping your workplace clean and organized – When your workplace is a mess, it is usually hard to look for things underneath the pile. Sometimes it takes hours for you to look for a lost paper on a cluttered pile. Therefore keeping things organized improves your over-all efficiency.

7. Setting Goals for yourself – Having practical and achievable goals for yourself is an important step in proper time management. Setting goals keeps you motivated to do your job well. Remember that you need efficiency to get things done the right way.

Exercises:
1. List 5 Time-wasters in your day.
2. List all the tasks in your day.
3. List all the time you relax during your day.

Personal Time Management Software

In a fast paced world, learning how to budget your time poses major advantages. Several tools like diaries, planners, and to-do lists, have been innovated to help assist in better time management efforts. While these traditional tools are still widely used, the technological advancements of our time has allowed for a more efficient way to deal with this.

Most of us today have access to the computer and the internet. And if these are used properly, they can be effective personal time manager. You can get several softwares in the market that you can use.

The following are just a few of the Personal Time Management Softwares that you can use:

Daily Planner Software

Daily Planners are usually bulky and hence can provide quite a discomfort on your part if you had to bring it with you at all times. Today, PDAs or Personal Digital Assistants help you arrange your schedules since it is equipped with a Management Software.

Most computers and PDAs nowadays are equipped with management softwares. And with the recent breakthrough in technology, it has also been made available in cell phones.

The software's task is simple. It is the same as the traditional analog planner, although with additional amenities. It automatically sorts your appointments according to date, alphabetical or numerical order. For better organizational procedure, you can even provide colour coding techniques to distinguish one project from another.

Its calendar system is more complicated. You will be able to configure your management software to start a countdown timer of events or a count-up timer as well. You can post these tools on your desktop for easy reference.

Aside from its basic organizer and calendar system feature, you can also create your to-do list on your desktop. Simply input them with the software and it will automatically appear on your desktop.

Free Time Management Softwares

Despite the convenience that a digital time management tool can provide, there is also a downside to this. Most time management softwares can become really expensive. So, if you are looking to save money then you might just stick with the traditional analog.

Don't despair just yet because the Internet provides the best alternative for you. There are several free time management softwares online.

If you are subscribed to a free e-mail service from either Google or Yahoo, you can take advantage of their increasing competition. Hence, they usually update or introduce new services to their subscribers. These services include online organizers, word readers, and spread sheet makers.

Gmail's online Time Management boasts a lot of features. Aside from the usual Calendar organizer that most e-mail has, it also has a document writer, reader and photo organizer. These features are already indispensable at this moment because even if you are not on your own computer you can already create and modify different documents, perfect for all types of people.

Google's Gmail is earning more popularity by introducing these kinds of services. Aside from the fact that it's free, the accessibility of creating your own organizer is of great convenience to everyone.

Meanwhile, Gmail also has an online time management software that includes several features. On top of the calendar organizer, there is also a document writer, reader, and photo organizer.

Those are just a few things that these Time Management Softwares can offer. As technology continues to advance and offer innovative softwares that respond to the needs of people, you can expect to use effective tools for better time management.

An Insight into Personal Time Management

If you were to ask successful people on how they achieved their status, most of them would cite proper personal time management. Although this concept is often mentioned in books or television, only a few realize what this is really all about. What exactly is time management? How you proper time management deliver the success you aspire?

Definition of Personal Time Management

You can define time management in several ways. It is usually associated with lots of things but the simplest way to define personal time management is using time to its maximum potential.

Personal time management works like economics. Its main objective is to allocate your scarce resource, which is time, properly so you can maximize the amount of work you can accomplish within a day. Since you cannot use the full 24 hours in a day to finish whatever you need to accomplish, proper allocation of time is critically important.

Problems that Arise With Poor Time Management

One of the biggest indicators of poor time management is last minute cramming to meet a deadline, rescheduling meetings because you forgot them, or not being able to do anything productive for the day. This leads to poor performance. Hence, you need to do something to address it.

Over confidence is one factor that can lead to poor time management. Oftentimes, we take too many workloads thinking that you can manage to do them with less effort. However, this only leads to inefficiency and waste of time.

With increased responsibility, you need to expand your efforts exponentially as well. If not, problems are very likely to arise and you have to become more efficient in meeting the demands of your work.

Poor time management results from people's false notion that they can do anything within a short period of time. However, they fail to foresee other factors that may affect their schedules.

What Does Proper Time Management Allow You to Do?

Practicing proper time management on your schedule is the best way to improve yourself. Eventually, you will take one step at a time on the ladder. Proper time management allows you to eliminate losses, plan each day effectively, allocate time for more important tasks, learn to refuse excessive workloads, and ensure that your long-term goals are not neglected.

These strategies, though not clearly understood by most people, will help you attend to your daily tasks. Meanwhile, it also improves the quality of your work output for that day. It is of utmost importance in the corporate world because every little time wasted also translates into waste of money.

Proper Personal Time management is like any other management process. It must be monitored and reviewed regularly. If you find out that there are flaws within your management process, this must be immediately addressed in order to achieve maximum efficiency.

Long term objectives are also emphasized in proper time management. Long term objectives are usually neglected due to the lack of specific deadlines. Plus the fact that it is considered a future goal, there is no pressure associated with it. However, in order for your Personal time Management to work, you must consider your long term objectives along with your daily goals.

Proper Time Management needs practice in order to be successfully applied in real life. It's not expected for you to change everything only in one night. Hence, when you spot discrepancies in your own time management skills, there is a way to deal with them. Efficient time management cannot be done overnight; it is a long-term process of learning until you have fully developed the skill of properly using your time.

Teaching Time Management Skills

Teaching time management skills is like any other form of teaching. When you teach a concept, it takes time before a student or the person is able to learn and fully develop that skill. Teaching the concepts is not enough, but you also need to follow up on your student to make sure that they regularly use whatever skill they have learned. That way, they make good use of it and be able to think of ways to enhance that skill. These are some time management skills that you can focus on when teaching your students.

1.) Prioritizing

Prioritizing is one of the basic concepts you must teach your student with regards to time management. This is because most people are hampered by too many activities at once. Many could fall into the idea of finishing a task just for the sake of it, not knowing that there are more important activities to attend to first. But the more crucial part here is identifying which ones should be top priority, because after all when it is in your list it should be important. Bottom line us, time management would depend on your own mental state of the amount of control you have of your time.

2.) Planning For Long-Term Time Management

You can also teach your students how to plan for long-term tasks and projects. Let them create a mind-set that enables them to project their lives months from now. As much as you want to establish the importance of their day to day activities, setting future goals are what drives your present activities.

Once they have realized the importance of future goals, they will understand the importance of being able to accomplish their everyday tasks. Hence, setting long-term goals and breaking them into smaller chunks (such as daily or weekly goals), you would gradually build that skill.

3.) Reviewing Daily Tasks

The third most important skill to master is the daily review of what just transpired within a given day. You must practice how to review and examine the work you accomplished for a day. Ask your students about what specific parts of the day were they able to manage their time efficiently, and which part of the day were they most unproductive. Hence, this will allow them to recognize the flaws in their own time management skills. Unless your students recognize them, they won't be able to fix them.

4.) Commitment To Higher Learning

Another major skill to teach your students is the ability to strive for learning and commitment to further improve their time management skill. It should be a continuous process. You can give them advices when it comes to time management careers, so they would know exactly where to go. As they learn new skills from time to time, they continue to improve themselves and advance their own time management skills.

Tell you students that their focus everyday should be on gradual and continual improvement of their time management skills. Once they have done this long enough, they should be able to form good habits that can lead them into even greater success in their lives.

Time Management Games

Before even attempting to play time management games, you have to bear in mind that it can be addicting. Hence, it is important to also learn how to manage your playing time. Also, when you download time management games, make sure they are from a website that you trust and are free of viruses. Therefore, you have to keep your anti-virus program updated.

There are many time management games online that can be played online or have a downloadable version of the game. There are many games from different categories but they would still fall on time management. You can try several of these time management games to find out which one you would like the most. Some of these games are listed here.

Diner Dash

This is a popular time management game that brings out the entrepreneur in all of us. In this game, you play as Flo who got tired of her desk job and was forced to start up her own restaurant business. Flo is now working on her own to get to the top.

The game is not as easy as it looks. Here, your time management skill will be put to the test as you have to wait on customers, deliver their orders, tell customers to sit down, and many others. As you progress from one level to the next, the game only gets harder.

Those who have previously played Diner Dash have noticed that it combines a fast paced puzzle action game with a "build your own restaurant" theme. For the first few levels of the game, you would start off as a greasy spoon run of the mill diner. And if you succeed, you can end up with Flo in her dream restaurant.

Diner Dash offers over 40 challenging levels to play that would progress you through 4 complete re-models of your restaurant. It also offers five different types of customers with each of them having specific behaviours. There is also a high score tracking and an automatic game save function so you can go back to the level where you left off.

Delicious 2 Deluxe

Another popular time management game is Delicious 2 Deluxe. This time, you take the role of Emily who needs to help her Uncle Antonio out of a financial fix. You need to help Emily by retrieving her family's finances in over five all new restaurants. You can use the income that you have earned while playing through the game to purchase decorations for your restaurant in order to bring in more customers. There are Emily's friends and family to help you get through with Emily's problem; but it would still take most of your help in order to retrieve Uncle Antonio's finances.

Delicious 2 Deluxe offers two game modes with over 60 challenging levels, plus five all-new restaurants with new customers. Plus, you can customize the restaurant's decorations according to your own preference.

These are just a couple of time management games that can be found on the internet. Playing time management games can help you experience and learn more time management techniques. Always remember though that these games can be addictive, so take a break once in a while from playing and return to your everyday work schedules.

Time Management In The Workplace

Ask yourself these questions:

• Am I working effectively?

• Is the work I do efficient?

• Do I have many fruitful hours of work or am I always distracted?

There are a number of time management tips to help you organize your office or workplace time more effectively and efficiently to get more out of your usual work day.

Workplace Time Management Tips:

1.) Purchase An Answering Machine Or Get A Secretary To Answer Your Phone Messages

Rather than being constantly being distracted by answering your telephone, hire a secretary or get an answering machine to take your phone messages for you. You can then set them aside at a certain point in the day to return those calls. Be breaking apart the time you spend doing your work and taking phone calls, you will be able to focus more clearly on the each task at hand so you can get more out of your time. Having and practicing effective time management skills would give you focus on the current important tasks. With this, an important time management tip would be to minimize distractions as much as possible, such as using the phone and the computer while working for e-mails.

2.) Make A To-Do List For The Days Ahead

You can sometimes see To-Do lists as a usual time management tip. Practicing effective time management skills and techniques on your workplace means that before you leave for the office or your workplace, you already have a prepared to-do list for the day. Hence you will easily be able to plan ahead your day. This way, once you enter your workplace you know exactly what to do in order to focus your attention on that.

3.) Do Things That Would Take 5 Minutes Or Less Immediately

Another time management skill in the workplace is that if you do a task that would only take you 5 minutes or less you need to that as soon as you receive it. When doing this, you will get the less important things out of the way immediately and you won't waste time thinking about doing it later.

4.) Keeping Your Workplace Clean And Organized

One of the major causes of ineffective time management, especially in the workplace, is not keeping your desk or office organized. Keep your office well organized, like keeping in places you have assigned them to and you won't waste your time searching for things that you need. Doing this also minimizes items from going missing as you would know exactly where you left them.

5.) Prioritizing

Setting and listing your major priorities is vital. Therefore, an important time management tip would be that you should and always know both long term and daily basis of what your priorities are.

6.) Dividing Your Workload

You don't have to do everything yourself. You can divide yours with other office personnel. This not only cuts time in terms of finishing your office workload but also makes it easier on your part. When you know someone in your workplace that can get the job done faster than you then you can delegate the load to that person.

7.) Setting Smart Goals

Setting goals that would be achievable, rewarding, specific, and timely would let you know what you are working towards for. Goals are useful in presenting to you what kind of steps you need to take in order to fulfill your dreams for the future.

Time Management Skills And The Brain

As we live in a high paced world, there are lots of busy people nowadays. In fact, some of them are multi-tasking, or holding two jobs at once. But no matter how busy a person may be, there are simple strategies to employ so you can gain the time you need. Creating an proficient time management technique is challenging but rewarding in the end. Some suggestions you could ponder on to get you into the right direction of managing your time effectively are:

1.) Improve Your Computer Literacy

In a world driven by technology, why not use it to improve your own time management skills? There are time management softwares that can help cut down on your energy and help organize your specific tasks and activities.

It is also advisable to learn some program shortcuts to dramatically save time such as when you are making a report or presentation. For example, you can use some keyboard hotkeys that you remember in order to make the report or presentation faster. It is much more efficient as opposed to reaching for the mouse and then looking for the icon to click on. There are various online beginner tutorials or workshops that can teach you these things within your desired areas of concern.

2.) Improve Your Creativity

Improve your creativity. This will allow you to build and develop more ingenious and creative ideas on how you can save time doing your work. Hence, a person becomes more productive and efficient throughout the day.

3.) Improve Problem Solving And Critical Thinking Aspects

When you improve your problem solving ability as well as critical thinking, you can spend less time on the thinking process. Instead of wasting your time to process your thoughts, you can use that to focus on finishing your task.

4.) Improve Delegation Skills

Learning and improving ways to delegate your work can also help you achieve good time management skills. It is good to have another pair of hands to help you with your tasks and projects. This will dramatically reduce the time you spend on doing your tasks. Once you learn how to properly delegate tasks, you can save time that you can use to focus on other pressing matters.

5.) Improve Your Emotional Intelligence

When you tend to become emotional with your work, you lessen your productivity. You lose your focus and even if you did complete your tasks, it is not of the quality you desire. Emotional intelligence encompasses the process of taking control of your emotions. Emotions can easily get in the way of your performance; so the lesser emotional distractions you can get, the better your performance at work is.

6.) Improve Your Multi-Tasking Abilities

By improving your multi-tasking abilities, you will be able to complete tasks in a shorter period of time. You can work with other people to further improve and develop your multi-tasking ability. You have to remember though that when you are doing tasks that require much attention and focus, it is best to avoid multi-tasking since you're at a risk of causing errors or mistakes.

7.) Taking Regular Breaks

Other than working many hours a day in a straightforward manner, always remember to take breaks in between tasks. This will avoid too much stress exerted on your body. You might notice that by the end of the day, you feel overly fatigued. When you take regular breaks, you refresh your body and mind. Hence, you are able to process more information and be more productive.

Time Management for Parents

For new parents, they face a common dilemma of making that much needed transition. If you do have work, you also need to juggle that along with your priorities in the family. You can probably easily manage the time at the office but the real challenge lies in organizing your household such as sending or picking the kids up at school, preparing dinner, or cleaning up the house. If not managed well, these tasks can prove stressful.

When you have kids for the first time, it is only natural to suffer from jitters especially with a new setup. However, the solution to this is simple. You just have to cope with your situation since it is only through experience that you'd be able to find a better approach to family life. But here are proven and trusted solutions that any parent might find useful.

Setting Priorities

Learning how to properly set priorities is among the most important skill that every parent, whether new or not, must practice especially for the working ones. The key here is to recognize the difference in schedule as compared to when you were on your own now that you have your kids as your main obligation. Then, you can make the appropriate changes.

You must be able to determine which is your top priority: is it your kids or your work? You have to remember that your decisions have trade-offs, therefore you would have to identify which of them has the least trade-off.

An additional tip that you can employ, you can also try setting up a "to-do" list for your set of activities within a day. That way, you can easily update what priorities you need to focus one.

Delegating other Duties

When it comes to work at home, it is usually the wives' responsibility to handle them. However, wives must not carry the sole burden of looking after the entire house. Instead, you can delegate other duties to your husband so you can have equal share of the workload at home.

If your husband is not acquainted with domestic chores, this is the best time to get him started. You can divide the chores at home such as washing the dishes, doing the laundry, or cleaning up the house. If not, then you can have him take care of the kids while you finish up on some chores. More than being able to accomplish the chores faster, it forms a bond and creates a healthier working relationship between both of you as parents.

If your kids are old enough, you can even ask them to help you out with the tasks at home. You can start with training them to fix their beds or clean up their rooms, as well as putting their dirty clothes into the laundry basket. Aside from the help they can provide you in maintaining your home, it also teaches them how to be responsible.

Planning out in Advance what you have to do

For mothers, it is best to plan ahead what you have set out to do for the following day. Among these things is creating a menu ahead of time. Therefore, when it is time to prepare lunch or dinner for the family, you already have an idea what to cook for them.

By creating a weekly menu, you increase your efficiency. After all, who has the time and energy to spend wondering about what to cook for dinner after an exhausting day at the office?

Delegate Proper Time for Shopping

When it comes to going out with your family, you need to also plan ahead your itinerary. This will help you prepare the things you will bring with you ahead and figure out if you have missed anything. Enough preparation will ensure that you will have all the things you need for this day off with the family.

As for shopping, there are a few simple tips that any mother would find useful. Shopping at the grocery usually takes a lot of time. Hence, you need to produce a list of the essential items you need to pick up. Not only will this help make shopping faster, but will also make sure that you do not forget anything. Or else you would eat up more time since you have to return to get the items you've missed.

For parents, time management usually entails mere common sense. And when you have properly set your priorities, you are good to go.

Time Management For Students

In today's world, we face a lot of distractions every day. The case is especially tough for a typical student who is struggling to create a balance between school and other societal factors that contribute to becoming a holistic individual.

Therefore, today's young generation is slowly losing their sense of time management. The dilemma lies in sifting through all these factors and setting their priorities. Without proper time management, a student could indeed fall behind and live an imbalanced life.

1.) Balance Between Work, Study, And Life

Contrary to popular belief, time management works simply. However, the hard part is being able to practice it and implant it within your subconscious to make it seem natural.

For a student, he or she must be able to classify time alloted for classes, working, studying, and partying. If you do not have a clear sense of what to do with your time, it is easy to go along with the flow and that is where poor time management all begins.

A student must be able to differentiate the various aspects of your student life, so there is always a separate time for everything. For instance, you have an upcoming quiz or exam, you must learn to cut down or eliminate partying from your schedule to allot more time for study. Indeed, for this method to be a success one must need only common sense.

However, some people tend to over estimate their capacity to manage their time. Hence, they end up consuming more time doing one task that they have none left for the other.

Learn how to adjust your schedule so you won't end up stressing out just trying to make up for lost time. If you have to, write down your schedule so you can keep track of where you need to be at a certain time.

2.) Time Portioning

Students might initially find doing school assignments and work projects boring and stressful. However, you can opt to divide the larger tasks into small, more manageable, tasks. That way, you won't find yourself eating up several hours of your time just trying to complete one task.

Another benefit for doing this is that you'd be able to allocate these smaller tasks into smaller time schedules that would have a definite start and end. Once you have completed those smaller tasks, you can move on to other tasks. Hence, it eliminates the boring factor as you continually alter your schedule instead of being stuck on one for hours.

3.) Reward For Managing Your Time

When you manage your time as a student, you can get some more free time to spare as rewards so you have more time to go to parties or just have a bit of fun. Remember that all work and no play would make a student very dull.

Nursing And Time Management

Nurses do their best to take care and provide sufficient health care services to people who need it. Nursing is defined as the care for the sick and maintenance of people's health as well. Nursing deals with the tasks of promoting growth, caring and feeding for infants and toddlers, preventing diseases, promoting good health, assisting in faster recovery, and promoting good health to their patients.

Nurses can employ several techniques in order to have effective time management. When they have successfully done that, it saves them from a lot of stress so they can be more productive and efficient. Some of these techniques are:

1.) Organizing And Planning The Days Ahead

Planning ahead your itinerary for the day and for the days ahead will make life easier for most nurses. The list is an effective time management tool that they can consult for what set of tasks they are scheduled to accomplish within a given day. This might seem really simple but it could spell the difference between a highly stressed day over an efficient one.

However, for the list to be effective it must be very specific. Include time frames for each set of activities or activity. Therefore, you will know whether you are spending so much time doing one thing instead of moving on to another task. The length of the list varies according to your preference, whether you want to create a list for the day or for the entire week.

2.) Avoid Distractions

Every day we face several distractions in our daily activities. Nurses are no exceptions. With so many distractions, it can lead to waste of time since it could be spent on unnecessary activities. Distractions can come in different forms, whether through taking lots of time on the phone, chatting with fellow nurses or hospital staffs, or watching television.

These are all unproductive activities that you can do without. And yet, they cause you to loss valuable time or even neglect your duties to your patients.

3.) Planning Daily Goals

Listing down your daily set of activities is not enough. You also need to have a set of goals that will aim to motivate you in doing or finishing your tasks. These goals will help nurses do their tasks more efficiently. It is not just a matter of completing your tasks, but you must also determine whether you have accomplish your goal.

4.) Thinking Positive

Positive thinking will help boost a nurse's performance at work. With it, they can follow their list of activities with better functionality. It can always be seen that optimism helps achieve better results. A nurse should teach one's self to strive harder on their task, to always perform better.

Nurses with proper time management skills and have lessen the stress they experience tend to have a more pleasing personality. Stress indeed can be your biggest adversary. Therefore, when you possess a more positive vibe, it enables you to communicate and work with your fellow nurses efficiently.

Time Management for Hospital Staff

A nurse and other hospital staff deal with and are responsible for a lot of things in a clinic, a hospital, or a place where their services are needed. They help treat, recover sick people with their acute or severe illnesses, maintain their patient's good health, and treat life-threatening illnesses and emergencies within a very wide range of health care practices. This is just among the many responsibilities of nurses, along with other health care professionals.

Indeed, a nurse's task is not only difficult but also complicated. Nurses are there to provide the doctor a lending hand when it comes to treating sick patients. Not only that, they also have to continually acquire new and innovative ways to provide the best form of treatment needed according to a patient's case. Some of these cases include caring for infants, promoting means to assist the growth of toddlers, or ways of preventing certain diseases. They work is critical because it is their patients' lives on the line, and so there's no room for error.

Nurses need lo learn a lot of various skills that are important for practicing their profession. With all these strenuous activities that nurses undertake every day, they would sometimes be unable to attend to other tasks at hand.

A nurse and hospital staff need to prioritize all their activities in order to provide more room for his or her other important daily activities. One way to be able to succeed in doing that is through effective time management skills.

Some suggested time management techniques that nurses should use include the following:

1.) Organize Your Activities For The Day

First of all when you are a nurse, you should note down the most important things that you should be doing for the day, and even in the days to come. You have to emphasize your top priorities, in case you need some things done first before the others. This will help organize your tasks so you can easily attend to them and finish necessary tasks on time. And with good management of time, you still have enough time left to do other useful activities.

2.) Focus And Prioritize

Prioritize on the most important tasks that are to be done and focus on them. Don't let yourself be distracted by things that would delay you and prevent you from finishing your tasks on time.

Avoid interruptions such as taking long chats with fellow nurses or patients so as not to delay the completion of your tasks. You can attend to less important activities after you are done with your shift or during free time.

3.) Avoid Less Important Activities

Avoid activities that would make you spend a lot of time. Among these things are watching television, taking long chats, sending e-mails on the internet, or taking too long conversations on the telephone. You may not realize it but a majority of your time is spent on less important things that you can probably do a day without. Although you can allot a few time for these, you should not spend substantial or valuable time on them.

Beyond better performance at your job, better time management helps lessen the stress in the life of nurses. This would then help them to better communicate with the people they are working with. And better communication at work increases your effectiveness and productivity at work.

Interesting Time Management Activities

Time management can be done by just about anyone. Most people would like to believe they have full control of their time. However, most of the time they are consumed by trying to fit in every priority into what little time they have. There will always be deadlines, whether it is imposed by events such as a flight schedule that would leave at a certain time, or by other people like your boss that asks you to do a project and he needs it by the end of the week.

How can you effectively manage your time when you only have control of a meagre percentage of your time? There are techniques that you can do to provide solution to this daunting question.

1.) Note Where You Spend Your Time

Try to have a log book or a "To-do" list where you can note down what you are doing and what else needs to be done. This will better help you manage your time, so you don't end up repeating tasks. Sometimes it would take longer for you to do this but this exercise will help you start off in managing your own time by highlighting where you are spending most of your time. Hence, you will be able to evaluate what you do and decide whether or not you need to change your time emphasis.

2.) Applying The 80/20 Rule

The 80/20 rule simply means that 80% of the results would come from the 20% of the time and effort that you use. Analyze and work on what you can do best that can guarantee the best results for your effort. Then, spend time doing that rather than doing some activities that are unproductive and can lead to delay on your work.

3.) Leaving Things Unfinished

This may sound like it's the opposite of time management but there are lots of things that can come across our paths that can be safely ignored and undone. Therefore, you can postpone them some other time. An example would be checking your e-mails whether or not it will arrive at your recipient or not. If it is really urgent, then you can ask for someone's help to take your place so you can make sure you still accomplish whatever needs to get done.

4.) Skipping The News

The daily news on the television will continue to happen whether you watch it for 30 minutes a day or not. You will find out that cutting out watching the news on the television has a good side effect of automatically cutting out lots of negativity in your life. This is like killing two birds with one stone as you also gain 30 more minutes to do your work.

5.) Learn To Say No

Perhaps one of the most effective time management techniques is practicing to say no to less important tasks and events. When you can say no, you gain an assertion technique that can and should be developed. When you can do this, you can finish the more important tasks earlier rather than putting them off at a later time. You will also avoid cramming just to get everything done on time.

6.) Hiring The Services Of Others

When you really need help to finish all the things you need to be done, you can always hire some help. For instance, you can hire cleaners for your home, or a gardener to look and keep your garden clean while you do your work. Entrust these less important tasks to the people you hired.

Time Management Courses

Time management is a useful tool any person can have and apply when leading a stressful lifestyle. With effective time management skills, you can have more time to finish your work on time, especially when you're trying to meet deadlines.

Time management courses can be found either online or offline. There are books that can be seen on your local book shop about effective time management techniques. Or you can read various helpful articles over the Internet about how to practice useful time management techniques.

When applying and taking these time management courses, you can achieve lots of benefits. Some of these benefits to learning and practicing these time management courses are:

- Do better with your work output and accomplish them with less effort and time

- Have enough time to focus on other equally valuable aspects of your life

- Leave you feeling fulfilled and satisfied with the effort you put in and the results you got

- Focus more time and energy on the things that are most important to you

- Plan and achieve your short and long-term goals

- Reduce idle time or wasted time so that you will have more productive output by the end of the day

- Get the job done while having reduced stress and anxiety

- Become excellent when it comes to time management in all aspects of your life

The following are tips and techniques that you can use if you want to establish more effective time management skills. Their success rate vary from one technique to the other but learning how to utilize these techniques to achieve desirable results would be worth the effort.

1.) How To Make A To-Do List

Most time management courses would teach you how to create an effective a to-do list that you can start using if you want to learn and practice effective time management. This is because when you have a to-do list, you do not have to rely on your own memory to remind you of what you need to do. You can consult on an actual list to keep track of tasks completed and those that you still have to finish.

2.) Learning How To Say No

Another time management course that you may come across is practicing how to say no. What this aims to teach you is better recognition of more important tasks. It teaches you how to effectively turn down or resist doing less important things when you are trying to beat a deadline. Aside from that, it also enhances your assertiveness.

3.) Thought Before Action

One of the skills that enhance your ability to manage your time well is learning how to think before acting on something. Hence, you will be able to avoid unnecessary actions that would slow your work down.

4.) Identifying Bad Habits

A good time management course is one that teaches you how to identify your undesirable habits. When we say bad habits, it means those activities that waste your time, sabotage your goals, and slow down (if not utterly block) your success. Thus, you need to break this bad habit by replacing them with healthy and time efficient ones.

Time Management Tips And Tricks

Properly allocating your time is never an easy task, especially if you've never been the type to make the most of your time. However, there are a lot of ways in order for you to start up and slowly integrate your whole system into practicing effective Time management methods.

Here are a few tips in order for you to successfully initiate your time management skills.

Keys To Successful Time Management

Before you can use some time management strategies in your schedule, there are a few key principles you have to understand first.

You need to be aware of your goals. Having proper awareness of what your goals are will assist you in properly prioritizing your activities for the day. It also helps you to get motivated and avoid distractions in between work.

You also need to develop a flexible schedule for yourself. It must be flexible enough to make sure that if you need to fill in other things aside from your usual schedule, you can still take care of them when you need to.

Tips To Successfully Utilize Your Time

Here are a few tips to successfully utilize your time

1. Examine your old habits and look for ways to change them. – When you learn that your habits are not conducive to proper time management, then it's about time that you start changing them. Bad habits are usually hard to change but when you're able to overcome it, the results are rewarding.

2. Put up reminders at home and office about your goals. – Usually when you're trying to pursue long-term goals, you slowly lose focus on them. Putting reminders everywhere would help you get reoriented with your goals motivating you to strictly follow your schedule.

3. Maintain a list of specific things to be done each day and set a top priority on that list. – Maintaining a list of things to be done everyday is a great way to start on successfully allocating your time properly. A checklist would help you to remember all the things that you need to do for the day and compel you to finish them at the end of the day.

Furthermore making a checklist would definitely help you to become a more responsible person. It is more than just a reminder, but is critical in how you follow that list to see if it effective for you.

4. Concentrate on one thing at a time. – Some people try to do all things at the same time. This happens because people need to do a lot of things but they do not have the luxury of time. Proper time management allows you to concentrate on one task at a time. When you feel that this task is more urgent than the other, then you must first focus on that task before moving on to the next most important task.

When you concentrate only on one task, the time needed to finish the job will significantly lessen giving you more spare time.

5. Enjoy what you are doing – When you enjoy what you are doing, it creates less stress. When you are not stressed, you are more likely to accomplish your tasks within a shorter time frame. Consequently, you will be able to do more in your typical working hours.

6. Continually look at ways of freeing up your time – It is important to try to free your schedule up. Looking for ways to free up your schedule improves the time spent on finishing up your activities. Remember that if you save a few minutes from each activity, and then you sum them all up, you'd realize that you have saved a lot of time.

Time Management Techniques in Business

In business, every second counts. Therefore, an efficient system must be adopted in your workplace. You must always ask yourself if you are doing things at maximum efficiency because if not, then maybe its time to change a few things in your system.

Here are a few tips and techniques to remember for you to effectively maximize the potentials of your business.

Setting Goals for your Business

Every business should start with a clear and attainable business goal. This will serve as your ultimate destination and it is your responsibility to control the wheel in order to reach that destination.

Aside from using it as your motivation, the goals you set will also help you in the production process. Set specific number of quotas for your workforce per day so that you will efficiently meet up your own quota. Just like with your goals, you have to make your everyday quota realistic enough so you won't be frustrated because you did not meet them.

Dividing the Workload

Even with starting business, an equal appropriation of the workload to your employees will enable to get all aspects of the business taken care of. By dividing workload to your employees, you each give them a specific task in which they can focus on and dedicate their time too. Theory supports that dedicated tasks improve the speed of efficacy of the entire system.

If you know anyone amongst your employees who you believe is best suited for a specific type of job, delegate him or her into doing that task. That way, you can ensure that you have the best person taking care of a particular aspect of your business.

Keeping the Whole Workplace Clean and Organized

Ineffective time management is often the cause of inefficiency in your workplace. More importantly, you also need to have a working environment that is conducive for work. Hence, you have to keep your workplace clean and organized to eliminate the time it takes looking for materials or papers you need. The time you wasted looking for a sheet of paper among thousands of papers could have been spent on more productive work.

Most businesses, especially the ones in the food industry strategically place their utensils and other materials needed for food processing in areas where they could easily be accessed. This improves the efficiency on time with regards to food preparation. The faster they can prepare the food, the more they can cater to their customers' needs. And when they have more satisfied customers, it will produce your much needed income.

Make a Specific List of Activities for the Day

What the List does for you personally also works on your own business or workplace. Setting a list of what to do for the day will make the work free-flowing. When you have a lot of priorities to think about, it is so easy to forget some of them. Hence, the list will serve as a little reminder of what other important tasks to attend to. This tip though only works on businesses that do not involve mass production.

Purchase an Answering Machine or Hire a Secretary

Answering phones usually eats up a lot of your time. Instead of using those precious minutes in propagating your own business, you waste it on talking to people who might not even had to do with your business.

Hiring a secretary to answer your phone calls can help you to fully focus on your work. The secretary will just list the names of all those who called and return their call if necessary. Remember that one of the best ways to proper time management is through reduction of distractions from your surroundings.

Time Management Strategies

Every one of us only have 24 hours in a day to work with. Hence, time management strategies allow you to accomplish more within a few hours, instead of having to extend your work on a single task for days. Here are a few strategies that you can apply to achieve that:

1.) List Down Your Activities

It need not be overemphasized that you have to learn how to prioritize your work. Meaning, you must set aside the less important tasks so you can focus on the more urgent ones. When you learn how to do this effectively, you can easily accomplish whatever it is you need to do within a shorter time. Make it a habit to write down a list of things to do. If you want to be really specific, break down all that you have to do within a day and in the order that you want them to get done.

As you list down your set of tasks to do, you have to identify which ones are long or short-term projects. Hence, you will be able to determine how much time you can allot for them within a day. A short-term task might be accomplished within, say a couple of hours. Meanwhile, for long-term tasks, you can try allotting 1 or 2 hours each day until when you intend to finish them. Hence, breaking down tasks would make it more efficient for you as you won't find it too strenuous.

2.) Allocating Time

Once you have your list, you now have to decide on how much time to allocate for each task or project you have set out to do for the day. Some tasks eat up a lot of time, so you have to be aware which are those. So as not to end up wasting so much time on one task, you have to provide time limits on each task so you can easily move on to the next.

When you do tasks in smaller chunks, it becomes a lot easier for you. Hence, you have eased yourself of the pressure. Instead, you can just focus on what you need to finish.

3.) Know What You Want To Accomplish

Your "to-do" list will serve as source of information for what your daily goals are. Hence, you can consult it to know what you have to do once you're through with one task.

There are a few questions that you can ask yourself: How much time are you willing to render for doing leisure activities? Are you willing to cut on the leisure time and appropriate more of them into your work so it can be more productive? Once you know what your goals are, you can use that as a motivation in order to finish the list that you have made.

4.) Don't Make Your List Of Actions Too Long

When making your list, productivity is always on top of your mind. However, you should not try to make your list too long. Most people have this tendency but that is a common misconception. Doing more work at one time is not always equal to being productive.

Start off with a short list of the most important things you have to accomplish. That way, you can easily prioritize them. When you have already completed those on top of the list, you can always add a new set of activities.

When you try to put too many activities on your list, it may become too overwhelming for you. You could easily end up having to do several unfinished tasks at once. But that is not advisable. If you can or if it is within the time limits you have indicated for a certain task, try to complete it first before moving on to work on another one.

Time Management 101 - The Basics

Time management can be interpreted in several ways. But it is commonly understood as proper allocation of time in terms of maximizing it by accomplishing more tasks. It could be applied to a lot of situations, whether in school, or work, and basically everywhere that requires something to get done within a certain period of time.

Time Management In Focus

With a lot of things to do in a span of 24 hours, most people have a difficult time setting their priorities and recognizing what are the things that must be done first. There are a lot of distractions in life that can take our attention away from far more important things. Eventually, most of us fail to maximize our use of time that we end up accomplishing nothing for the day. Hence, the big question is: how do you manage your time?

Time management works very much like economics. It is an allocation of scarce resources, which in this case is time, in order to reap maximum efficiency at the end of the day. However, we don't need to become good economists in order to efficiently manage our time. All we need is common sense and good sense of judgment in order to maximize everything we do.

Things To Consider For Proper Time Management

In order to properly manage your time, there are a few things that you have to consider. You have to condition yourself to do the most important or most urgent tasks first. This is what sets responsible people apart from those who aren't. Knowing what things to prioritize first will help you to overcome all those distractions along the way.

However, recognizing your priorities is just mainly your first step. As the cliché goes, it is easier said than done. It is best recommended to list down the things you have to do for the day. When you already have the checklist or to-do list for the day, you have to create a mind-set wherein you must fulfil them. Once you are used to this list, soon you will get used to this that you do not even have to keep listing them. Instead, you'd create a mental note for what you are set to do for the rest of the day.

By doing this, you are not only able to set your priorities but develops a sense of responsibility that will prove helpful in the long run.

Knowing what your priorities are is just the first step. Relaxation is also an important factor in our everyday activities. The best thing to do is to initiate periodic rest times ideally 10 minutes every 2 hours in order to relax our mind and muscles from the stressful. Relaxing once in a while also improves our concentration in what we are doing. Hence, it improves your level of productivity.

Advantages of Time Management

There are a lot of advantages when we properly manage our time but we will just discuss a few and most important ones.

It eliminates cramming – When you have properly set your priorities, you are able to finish your task early. This cuts time and you'd be more likely to accomplish things in advance. Hence, you avoid cramming. When you do your work earlier than usual it also follows you to achieve better results because you could allocate more time to focus on your task.

Eliminates stress – When you keep on beating deadlines, there is the tendency to use up more time. When this happens, you disrupt your sleeping habits and thus produce more stress. Proper Time management helps you eliminate the stress because you properly allocate your time for work and rest.

Proper allocation of your time is a hard task, but once you get used to it, you are sure to become more productive.

Useful Time Management Tools

While technology is at its most advanced state today, there remains to be a lot of things to juggle for a typical career-oriented individual. For most family-oriented people, there is the burden of juggling work, career, family and other factors involved in one's social life.

The answer is Time Management. Most successful people are often asked about what their secret to success is. And more often than not, they have the same response, and that is "time management". However, although this is almost an expected response, many are still baffled at how time management really works.

Time management is simply the proper allocation of time for certain priorities. First, the priorities have to be arranged in a certain way where it is clustered into sectors and listed according to urgency and importance. For example, the important parts of your life are career, your son, your home, your art, and your family. You have to know which one to drop first whenever you need to do something.

After that, you will need help from some time management tools designed to aid you in the correct process of prioritization AND remembering that order.

Quick-and-Easy Reminders

There are a lot of people who need lots of reminder when it comes to taking care of small businesses. Often, they are too small that they are disregarded as unimportant. If you are one of them, buy some quick-and-easy reminders. What's good about technology is you can probably put a reminder just about everywhere! Cellular phones nowadays have built-in organizers, post-its are available in different variants, and even the good old refrigerator door magnets have come in a lot of forms.

What is important is that the frequency of the reminding is now being increased. This is good for time management because it keeps you aware of the things which you have to do especially if they're urgent.

The Organizer + Watch Tandem

These are staples for just about every busybody – from the college beadle to the corporate leader. The organizer is something that holds your appointments and it's also a tiny little space for some writing. Busybodies usually have contact numbers of random people they meet, gifts for a not-so-relevant birthday party that he has to go to or some sudden brilliant ideas that come to mind. For these and more, you will need an organizer. It has to be a little notebook, just enough to fit in a handbag, and should be made of durable material. You must bring your organizer with you every day, in case you need to list something down as a reminder.

Moreover, the perfect complement to an organizer is a high-quality watch. You may have experienced running late for an appointment just because your watch didn't work well. What's worse is that the person you're meeting wouldn't even believe you. This blunder can easily be avoided. Just get a high quality watch. Having a good sense of time is practically the first step in time management.

The Perfect Mindset

It's pressuring to know that you have a lot of things in your hand and it seems like you can't even do anything about it. Don't tip over.

Moreover, keep a "be on your toes" kind of mindset as you maneuver your way into your busy life. Sure, there are times when you distance yourself from your organizer. For some, it is a painful reminder of the busy life they lead. It's perfectly alright to feel some form of eternal urgency but take some time off once in a while. You must never neglect yourself in your list of priorities.

Time Management Training

People nowadays need to get a lot of things done especially with regards to their job. However, they tend to lose track of a lot of events and end up incurring losses in time. The problem is that these losses are unnecessary and are therefore not advisable if you have a job.

At its core, the problem is in terms of poor time management. How many times have you faced the dilemma of having too many meetings in one day or trying to beat an impossible deadline? And the worse thing is, you get too stressed out that it overflows into your personal life. You manage to rub off that stress onto your family members and that is when it becomes unhealthy.

The key to solving such problems is a proper time management program. With it, you can help yourself avoid unnecessary risks when it comes to your job. It may even help prevent losses outside of the job.

The program

Although it rests on an simple concept, time management is a lot more complicated than it seem. There are special training programs that you have to undergo in order to avail of the full benefits of proper time management. It is not enough that you understand the basic concepts of time management. You also need to know how to apply them so everything you've planned on doing won't end up a disaster. If not, then you could easily wind up committing more mistakes as you don't know the limitations of the basic concept.

That is what time management training is for. It allows you to have a better grasp with regards to time management. Then you will know what kind of timetable you need to have in order to maximize productivity levels within and outside of your job sphere.

Hence, there are trainings for time management.

The benefits

Most people fail to realize that the major cause of losses in terms of productivity and efficiency at work is because of stress. On the other hand, stress is a result of the worries over matters related to one's job. Therefore, stress is your biggest adversary in all of these.

Time management training gives you a chance to know what level of stress you are capable of handling. Hence, it allows you to determine what type of job you should accept. When you are aware of all these, you will be able to stay within your optimum productivity and efficiency levels without compromising your work schedule.

Time management training helps individuals manage stress. When you are able to manage your level of stress, you will also be able to lessen whatever losses you might incur during difficult times. This is of utmost importance because in order to stay competitive, you have to keep your productivity level at a maximum. This not only applies to your professional life though but also with your personal life.

When you undergo this training, you will have a clearer idea on how to create an effective timetable and time management program on your own. Hence, you can determine whether to accept or defer calls for help from your officemates. This will have its own implication in terms of the working relationship within your workplace. This will allow each member of the team to boost their efficiency levels with their individual tasks.

Focus is one of the most important lessons you will learn with the training program. It allows people to assess which part of their lives to focus on at different times. This means that it allows individuals to live a full and healthy life despite being in a stressful, or rather busy, job.

The biggest gain you can take away with you by undergoing this kind of training is the emphasis on producing efficient work at your job. You cannot be efficient if you do not know your own limitations. You can easily overwork yourself, but that does not automatically mean you are being productive. Therefore, you need to practice such a program in order to gain maximum benefit from your job.

Important Time Management Websites

Mind-Tools
http://www.mindtools.com/pages/main/newMN_HTE.htm

Time Management Tips, Tricks and Strategies
http://www.businessballs.com/time.htm

Personal Time Management for Managers
http://www.ee.ed.ac.uk/~gerard/Management/art2.html

Time Management for Teachers
http://www.alice.org/Randy/timetalk.htm

Time Management for Students
http://www.counselingcenter.illinois.edu/?page_id=123

ABOUT THE AUTHOR
Warren Brown is an Amazon published Author, freelance writer, journalist, copywriter, proof-reader, Law of Attraction Practitioner and Life Coach.
http://www.publishsuccess.com

http://warrenbrown.blogspot.com

Email: info@publishsuccess.com

Researched, compiled and Edited by Warren Brown.

Copyright @Warren Brown

ISBN 978-1-291-22097-1

London. United Kingdom.2012